Elementary School Teaching Practices

Elementary School Teaching Practices

RUBY H. WARNER

Professor of Elementary Education
University of Miami

42075

1962

The Center for Applied Research in Education, Inc.

Washington, D.C.

Library of Congress
Catalog Card No.: 62–13616

Printed in the United States of America
27264

Foreword

There are many factors which determine what are, and what we believe should be, teaching practices in our elementary schools. Among these determining factors are our concepts of the nature of knowledge, our understandings about how children learn and develop ways of behaving, our beliefs about the principles of democracy—especially about the dignity and worth of the individual—the imperative that each be appropriately educated to maximum self-realization, and, finally, our notions about what subject matter is most appropriate and worthwhile. Whereas there is an historic continuity in our elementary school curriculum and teaching practices, changes in our basic understandings and beliefs are ultimately reflected, usually slowly, in changes in school practices.

The author of this book has taken a long look at the road by which our public schools have come to be what they are, thus providing a perspective from which to view the advances made by our elementary schools. She has advocated a sensible balance in school practices between the needs of the individual and the needs of society. She has taken the modern view that healthy self-realization of the individual is indispensable to good human relations in the world. She has emphasized that those practices that meet the needs of our democratic society, with its stress on the worth of the individual and his responsibility as a citizen, are likely to survive.

The author brings to her task the rich experiences of a long career in elementary education. She has lived through and played an important part in many of the changes in practice about which she writes. Her analysis will prove stimulating both to the professional educator who may wish to review with her the development and present status of teaching practices in the elementary school and also to the interested layman who may seek a better understanding of our elementary schools.

JOHN R. BEERY

Dean, School of Education

University of Miami

Contents

CHAPTER I

Foundations of Teaching Practices

Schools are dynamic institutions that reflect the culture in which they exist. In every period of history schools teach the customs, the mores, and the ideals of the culture. Our culture is not static but swiftly changing. Occasionally the transition is so abrupt as to be kaleidoscopic, so shaken are the pieces before a new design emerges. The factor that is hastening the change is technology. Stresses and strains and conflicting ideas exist in the period of adjustment. One would expect the school to feel this conflict in ideas and values, and so it does. The school in today's dynamic culture is not only expected to adjust to the culture but to help the culture adjust to technological change.

When our civilization was largely rural, children attended school for a few months in the winter when they were not needed to help on the farms. Teachers of this early era were inspired to fit the pupils for the simple life of the times and to teach reading, writing, and arithmetic so as to prepare pupils to become merchants, artisans, and farmers. Through these subjects, children learned the known basic knowledge which was fondly called the "social heritage." The prevailing method for insuring retention of that knowledge was drill. Teachers assigned lessons and heard recitations. If they were authoritarian in their methods, it was because the culture was authoritarian. The age was one of acceptance and not of doubt.

The teacher had only a few years in which to impart knowledge, for the majority of children attended only the grammar school, as the elementary school was then called, and many pupils did not finish the entire eight years of that school. The teachers themselves had comparatively little education. Only rarely were they graduates of a university.

With the coming of the industrial revolution and the migration of people from the farms to towns and cities, a new type of school had to arise to meet the changing needs of the culture. In one century, knowledge expanded so rapidly that it became impossible for one man to inherit all knowledge during his schooling or even during his

1

entire lifetime. The question then rose as to what knowledge was of most worth, and the final answer has not yet been found.

Today the importance of science to our very survival forced the schools to teach this subject. Social thinkers rightly argued that along with science we had to teach children a sensitivity to human welfare. Therefore, the social studies found a place in the curriculum. One by one, other subjects were introduced—art, music, health, safety, and foreign languages.

The schools, like society itself, were now definitely progressing away from the horse-and-buggy days and the rule of the hickory stick and the blackboard pointer.

What is ahead? With increasing automation, no one knows precisely what changes will be made in our ways of living. The possibility of a four-hour work day and more time for leisure will undoubtedly have its impact upon the school program. Methods of instruction now in use will give way to newer methods that better meet the needs of citizens of the future. Schools of today that pride themselves on their progressive methods will become traditional schools in the eyes of educators of the twenty-first century.

Traditional and Progressive Education

The terms *traditional* education and *progressive* education need clarification. Traditional education refers to teaching-and-learning methods of the past. Progressive education is education that moves ahead to adjust to new needs in society and includes research findings in psychology, sociology, philosophy, and other areas of knowledge.

Whenever an innovation is made, whether in the community or the school, enthusiastic devotees of the new method may for a time forget the advantages that lie in traditional methods and go overboard in exclusive use of the new. Eventually a balance is struck so that the good of both methods is preserved.

Early in the twentieth century a radical departure from traditional methods revolutionized teaching in certain schools. Today almost every public school has incorporated some of the procedures of those revolutionary changes into its classrooms. The new educational revolution was called progressive education. A group of educators interested in spreading knowledge about the newer methods and the philosophy that lay behind them was called the Progressive Education Association. Possibly the advertising of the changes to be wrought in the schools was too sensational and the change too rapid. Be that as it may, the term *progressive education* fell into disrepute in some circles and the new education was vilified in the press and on public platforms. In spite of these attacks, those aspects of method which were necessary to the best welfare of boys and girls still persist in all good schools.

Objectives of the Elementary School

In the United States the control of schools has never been centralized. The local communities have largely determined the types of schools that have existed, and one can, therefore, find a great diversity in aims and objectives.

As our first public schools were more or less fashioned after European models, some of our first purposes and methods were imported. Four great European philosophers made contributions of such magnitude that these contributions are still traceable in our schools today, although so interwoven that it would be almost impossible to separate the strands. These four great men were Rousseau, Pestalozzi, Herbart, and Froebel. Rousseau and Froebel emphasized the individualistic goals of education; Pestalozzi and Herbart, the social ends.

One of the early lists of objectives in this country was the "Cardinal Principles of Secondary Education"[1] which, although expressly formulated for secondary education, greatly influenced teaching and learning in the elementary schools. The stated purposes were health, worthy home membership, worthy use of leisure, vocational efficiency, ethical character, and good citizenship.

Many of the separate states issued their own courses of study with accompanying statements of purpose. One of the first of these was the Virginia Course of Study[2] which reads: "The learning experience which promises results in terms of modification of behavior occurs in the problem-solving setting, in which abilities and knowledge find purposeful use, rather than in the memorization of isolated facts and the mastery of unrelated activities."

The Virginia curriculum outlined certain functions of social life

[1] Commission on Reorganization of Secondary Education, "Cardinal Principles of Secondary Education" (Washington, D.C.: U.S. Bureau of Education, Bulletin No. 35, 1918).

[2] Tentative Course of Study for Virginia Elementary Schools (Richmond: Virginia State Board of Education, 1943), p. 498.

as the framework of the curriculum: personal development; protection and conservation of life; property and natural resources; production, distribution, and conservation of goods and services; consumption of goods and services; communication and transportation of goods and people; recreation; expression of esthetic and religious impulses. For the junior-high school, these two functions were added: education and extension of freedom.[3]

A widely accepted statement of educational policies in our American democracy was formulated by the Educational Policies Committee of the National Educational Association. The four major objectives are (1) self-realization, (2) human relations, (3) economic efficiency, and (4) civic responsibility. These are broken into explanatory sub-headings as follows:

THE OBJECTIVES OF SELF-REALIZATION

The Inquiring Mind. The educated person has an appetite for learning.

Speech. The educated person can speak the mother tongue clearly.

Reading. The educated person reads the mother tongue efficiently.

Writing. The educated person writes the mother tongue effectively.

Number. The educated person solves his problems of counting and calculating.

Sight and Hearing. The educated person is skilled in listening and observing.

Health Knowledge. The educated person understands the basic facts concerning health and disease.

Health Habits. The educated person protects his own health and that of his dependents.

Public Health. The educated person works to improve the health of the community.

Recreation. The educated person is participant and spectator in many sports and other pastimes.

Intellectual Interests. The educated person has mental resources for the use of leisure.

Esthetic Interests. The educated person appreciates beauty.

Character. The educated person gives responsible direction to his own life.

THE OBJECTIVES OF HUMAN RELATIONSHIP

Respect for Humanity. The educated person puts human relationships first.

---

[3] *Ibid.,* p. 523.

Friendship. The educated person enjoys a rich, sincere, and varied social life.

Cooperation. The educated person can work and play with others.

Courtesy. The educated person observes the amenities of social behavior.

Appreciation of the Home. The educated person appreciates the family as a social institution.

Homemaking. The educated person is skilled in homemaking.

Democracy in the Home. The educated person maintains democratic family relationships.

The Objectives of Economic Efficiency

Work. The educated producer knows the satisfaction of good workmanship.

Occupational Information. The educated producer understands the requirements and opportunities for various jobs.

Occupational Choice. The educated producer has *selected* his occupation.

Occupational Efficiency. The educated producer succeeds in his chosen vocation.

Occupational Adjustment. The educated producer maintains and improves his efficiency.

Occupational Appreciation. The educated producer appreciates the social value of his work.

Personal Economics. The educated consumer plans the economics of his own life.

Consumer Judgment. The educated consumer develops standards for guiding his expenditures.

Efficiency in Buying. The educated consumer is an informed and skillful buyer.

Consumer Protection. The educated consumer takes appropriate measures to safeguard his interests.

The Objectives of Civic Responsibility

Social Justice. The educated citizen is sensitive to the disparities of human circumstance.

Social Activity. The educated citizen acts to correct unsatisfactory conditions.

Social Understanding. The educated citizen seeks to understand social structures and social processes.

Critical Judgment. The educated citizen has defenses against propaganda.

Tolerance. The educated citizen respects honest differences of opinion.

Conservation. The educated citizen has a regard for the nation's resources.

Social Application of Science. The educated citizen measures scientific advance by its contribution to the general welfare.

World Citizenship. The educated citizen is a cooperating member of the world community.

Law Observance. The educated citizen respects the law.

Economic Literacy. The educated citizen is economically literate.

Political Citizenship. The educated citizen accepts his civic duties.

Devotion to Democracy. The educated citizen acts upon an unswerving loyalty to democratic ideals.[4]

This statement of educational objectives is one of the most important educational documents of the twentieth century. Both the growth of the individual and the social objectives are emphasized. Through this approach, basic skills and broad general knowledge is offered as the avenue to self-realization. The all-inclusive development of the individual embraces human relationships in the family, the community, and the world.

In the nineteenth century, educational literature and curriculum building centered upon the social aims of education. A twentieth century emphasis has been upon the child and his developmental activities. With the depression years of the 30's and with two World Wars, the social aim came again into the foreground. At mid-century education recognizes the interrelation of aims that seek to improve both the individual and the society.

Recently, education has shown a mental hygiene point of view that is aimed at prevention of behavior difficulties. In order to have a healthy personality, five vital needs of the self should be met: affection, belonging, cooperative living, creating, and a sense of achievement. The Mid-century White House Conference on Children and Youth accented these needs in its pledge to children:[5]

> From your infancy we give you our love, so that you may grow with trust in yourself and in others.
>
> We will recognize your worth as a person, and we will help you strengthen your sense of belonging.
>
> We will respect your right to be yourself and at the same time understand the rights of others, so that you may experience cooperative living.

---

[4] Adapted from Educational Policies Commission, *The Purposes of Education in American Democracy* (Washington, D.C.: National Education Association, 1938), pp. 50, 72, 90, and 108.

[5] Federal Security Administration, The Mid-century White House Conference on Children and Youth, *Final Recommendations and Pledge to Children* (Washington, D.C.: G.P.O., 1951).

We will help you to develop initiative and imagination, so you may have the opportunity freely to create.

We will encourage your curiosity and your pride in workmanship, so that you may have the satisfaction that comes from achievement.

All through our history, a continuing aim of education has been the teaching of the ideals of democracy. One of the earliest stated aims was to induct the newcomer to our shores into the American ideal and to pave the way for greater equality of opportunity. As with all dynamic ideas, the concept of democracy has grown with changes in society. Democracy to our pioneers meant the guarantee of certain civil liberties, among them freedom of speech, freedom of the press, and freedom of religion. In the twentieth century (in the Atlantic Charter) two other freedoms were added: freedom from fear and freedom from want. Included in the ideals of democracy are the inherent worth of the individual and the right of all individuals to equality of opportunity.

In order that the individual acquire and maintain the feeling of his own worth, the school must give him a feeling of adequacy and competence; it will therefore reject any method of instruction that makes the pupil feel inferior. The pupil's talents will be encouraged and creative expression will be practiced so that he may find his own unique personality. The maturing individual will become more sensitive to all violations of the principle of equality—to injustice, poverty, and persecution of minority groups. In spite of numerous failures in actual practice, democratic ideals have persisted throughout our history, and the challenge to education is to bring about their more complete fulfillment.

European Antecedents to Learning
Practices in American Elementary Schools

To four great Europeans, American elementary education owes a lasting and loving debt of gratitude—to Jean Jacques Rousseau, Johann Heinrich Pestalozzi, Johann Friedrich Herbart, and Friedrich Froebel. Although it would be possible to trace many other educative influences upon our schools, only the more direct and immediate influences will be discussed.

In the early training of teachers in the United States, the history of education occupied a preeminent place, and teachers were inspired by the biographies of great educators. Later, in the second decade of the twentieth century, this history was often abbreviated in courses in "Foundations of Education" which included not only the history but the psychology, philosophy, and sociology of education.

Jean Jacques Rousseau. One of the most influential social and educational reformers of the eighteenth century was Jean Jacques Rousseau (1712–1778). His social writings are credited with helping to bring about the French Revolution. His educational writings had an immediate effect upon the upbringing of children of his own day and a long-range influence upon a long line of distinguished educators that include Pestalozzi, Herbart, Froebel, and Dewey.

Born in the eighteenth century when educational institutions from local schools to universities were in a state of decadence, Rousseau exerted a profound influence upon education. Most of the common people of his day received no education. Such schooling as existed was finished by the child at age ten or eleven at the latest.

France was in complete subjection to Louis XIV. Freedom of speech was virtually unknown. The lower classes were in abject poverty. In the mounting revolt against the decadence, Rousseau's ideas fed the social and educational unrest.

Rousseau's birthplace was Geneva. His mother died at his birth and he was brought up by a father who neglected him. Rousseau drifted from occupation to occupation until he succeeded at writing. At the age of twenty-five, he came into contact with several stimulating French authors. In 1749 he entered an essay contest on the subject "Has the progress of the sciences and the arts tended to the purification or the corruption of morals?" He wrote on the latter side of the question and won the prize. The publication of his essay brought him fame. An essay on the cause of inequality among men followed and later a series of novels and romances that dealt with natural man. One of the novels, *The New Heloise,* had over seventy editions by the end of the century. His principal social work was *The Social Contract* in which he protested against the enslavement in which man everywhere found himself.

Rousseau's educational classic, which immediately became a bestseller throughout France, was *Emile.* It was eagerly read by ladies of fashion as well as by savants in the universities. Perhaps no other book in educational history has been more influential than this one. Whereas children had been previously considered to be innately evil, Rousseau went to the opposite extreme and wrote that they were innately good. This new concept of childhood led to an improved treatment of children in countless homes and schools.

Another of Rousseau's doctrines was that a child should be educated through his own explorations of the environment. A better education, he believed, could be obtained through physical activity and perception of nature rather than through books. The child must not be fitted into a sociological and theological mold. Rousseau believed children should have the freedom to behave and develop naturally. This theory has been called naturalism and its key ideas are growth, experience, and interest. These ideas were later repeated and developed by twentieth century educators.

The book *Emile* is divided into four chapters about the education of boys: infancy, childhood, boyhood, and adolescence. The fifth chapter concerns the education of Sophie, the girl Emile was to marry.

Emile had a tutor who arranged the environment to meet the individual needs of his pupil. To illustrate, the tutor one morning endeavored to teach Emile about the points of the compass but found little interest from Emile. They went for a walk in a vast park and lost their way. Emile was getting hungry as it was well past the dinner hour. Now he began to recall all that he knew about direction and was ready for further instruction. With the new instruction given him by his tutor, he reasoned his way out of difficulty.

Knowledge was not the chief aim of this manipulation of the environment but the desire and the taste for knowledge. Many of Rousseau's ideas that seemed revolutionary in the eighteenth century are now modified and practiced in American schools of the twentieth century.

Heinrich Pestalozzi. Pestalozzi (1746–1827) warmly acknowledged Rousseau's profound inspiration upon his own writings and teachings, but much of his educational theory grew out of his own practical experience in teaching.

Pestalozzi was born in Zurich, Switzerland and attended the university there. He tried several professions before becoming a teacher and writer. After experimenting with the education of his son Jacques, he opened a farm school at Neuhof with twenty neglected children. The children worked in the fields in summer and learned spinning and weaving and the 3 R's in the winter. They received affection instead of the cruelty which was the common discipline of that day. Pestalozzi believed that children would become moral by acting morally. He carefully observed each individual to see if the child gave evidence of health and well-being. In the five years of the operation of the Neuhof school, one hundred children were educated there. Then Pestalozzi doubled the number of pupils and found himself forced to close because of financial difficulty. Although not a success from the economic viewpoint, the school was highly successful in pointing the way to a better education for children in general and delinquents in particular. The example furnished by this school was followed in other countries.

During the next twenty years Pestalozzi wrote pamphlets and books on education and other topics, and among these was his famous novel of a decadent village *Leonard and Gertrude*. Gertrude was a mother who taught her children the domestic arts and at the same time talked to them about their own lives and how best to live. The children learned to count and measure through practical use of numbers as in counting the threads for spinning. Gertrude said of her method that it was all well and good for children to learn something, but the really important thing was for them to be something.

Schoolmen from the village came to visit Gertrude and her children, and a school was established in the village to employ methods similar to those used by Gertrude. Eventually the whole life of the village was reformed.

Another book, *How Gertrude Teaches Her Children,* was published nineteen years after *Leonard and Gertrude* and embodies Pestalozzi's ideas on education. He maintained that knowledge of a child's nature was essential to the best instruction. The methods of instruction could vastly aid or retard education. Discipline was to be strict but kind. The most valuable lessons were to be learned through direct experiences with objects and places, and through observation, inquiry, and reasoning.

An English adaptation of the Pestalozzian method was introduced into the United States by Edward A. Sheldon at the Oswego Normal School. The method was called *object teaching.* Through a thorough campaign of publicity, Dr. Sheldon made object teaching the most popular subject in educational conferences and writings from 1861 to 1880. Each lesson introduced a real object into the classroom. A description of the object was part of the procedure. Questions relating to the object were asked and answered. An activity program followed in which the pupil reproduced the experiences of the day's lesson. Other normal schools adopted the Oswego interpretation of Pestalozzi's method. The chief criticism of the object lesson is perhaps the isolation of one lesson from another and the lack of relatedness to larger themes. Also, the teacher dominated instruction so that there was very little pupil-purposing.

After object teaching declined, the remaining Pestalozzian influences were pupil activity to an extent formerly unknown, constructive and creative work, and pupil discussion.

Johann Friedrich Herbart. Johann Friedrich Herbart (1776–1841), sometimes called the "father of modern psychology," was a German philosopher and educator whose ideas gave an impetus to education in the first half of the nineteenth century. He became a lecturer on pedagogy at the University of Göttingen. He occupied the chair of philosophy at the University of Königsberg where he made education into a college course. Another pioneering effort was the establishment of a laboratory school where his college students could observe children who were being taught according to his methods.

The early writings of Herbart show his appreciation of Pestalozzi, whom he had met in Switzerland, but he became more critical of Pestalozzi's views as he developed his own ideas about education. His most important works were *Application of Psychology to the Science of Education* and *The Outlines of Educational Doctrine.*

Herbart was in rebellion against memoriter learning. He believed that a mere accumulation of facts was useless and that facts must be taught so as to have meaning for the learner. This learning should lead to character formation. He maintained that the aim of education was ethical and moral. He thought the most important school subjects in character formation were history and literature. These two subjects were to be used as a "core" for the curriculum and attention was to be concentrated upon them. Other subjects were to be correlated with history and literature so as to produce a unity of subject matter. Herbart's emphasis upon the importance of history as a subject for study influenced the introduction of social studies into the elementary school. Literature began to replace the material formerly used in the grade readers. Herbart anticipated the later use of *units of work* in the schools.

Some of the main planks in Herbart's educational platform were apperception, the culture-epoch theory, and his doctrine of interest.

The principle of apperception was that a new experience for the learner had to make contact and find some relationship with that which was already part of the learner. In other words, a new experience gets meaning from previous experiences to which it is related. In teaching, children should be prepared for new knowledge by first recalling relevant past knowledge. The principle of apperception is still regarded as sound psychology.

According to the culture-epoch theory, children live through stages similar to those of the race. This theory no longer appears in modern books on psychology.

Herbart's doctrine included not only interest as motivation but also interest as an end of education. Before knowledge, there must be interest and this could be obtained by a recall of the child's past related experiences. A many-sided interest should be developed, and therefore the curriculum should include not just a few but a wide range of subjects. This variety of interests should also possess a unity. Herbart believed this unity could be achieved through reflection and could be greatly aided by a correlation of subject matter.

Herbart's disciples outlined the Herbartian method into five formal steps of the recitation. These steps are preparation (a recall of old ideas in the learner's experience to which the new instruction can be related); presentation (a story, demonstration, experiment, or a reading assignment that included the facts or ideas of the new material); comparison (connections and associations between the old and the new); generalization (general principles that are formed from the lesson); and application (putting the new idea to work as in illustrating or recreating it).

Lessons based upon the five steps gave new life to classroom method. In the hands of skillful teachers the recitation was often vivid and thought-provoking. In other hands the five steps were followed as a dull routine or a teacher-dominated procedure. Too often no continuity existed between lessons, and the operation of the formal recitation became mechanical.

During the last half of the nineteenth century, students from America who attended the universities of Leipzig and Jena introduced Herbartianism into the United States on their return. One of these was Charles de Garmo, who became professor of education at Cornell University and served as the first president of the Herbart

Society. Another American disciple of Herbart was Charles A. McMurry of the Illinois State Normal University and his brother, Frank M. McMurry, both of whom had studied at Jena. The two McMurrys published *Method of the Recitation* in 1897, and Charles A. McMurry followed this text with other books on method for the elementary school.

Herbart's followers helped organize the Herbart Club in 1892, and this club became the National Herbart Society for the Scientific Study of Education in 1895. This name was again changed in 1902 to the National Society for the Scientific Study of Education.

Friedrich Wilhelm August Froebel. Froebel (1782–1852), a German educator, is famed as the father of the kindergarten. He was neglected in his early years and his memories of the sufferings of those years made him want to help children lead happier lives.

From 1805 to 1807 Froebel taught in a Pestalozzian school in Frankfurt. During the next two years he was both student and teacher at Pestalozzi's Institute at Yverdun. After studying at the University of Göttingen and at the University of Berlin, and serving a brief enlistment in the Prussian army, he instructed five nephews in a school which was conducted on the Pestalozzian principles.

In Switzerland he conducted several schools. He opened his first kindergarten in 1837 and later established other kindergartens and training schools for teachers. Kindergartens spread in most European countries except Germany, where in 1852 it was prohibited for a period of ten years.

Froebel introduced play into the kindergartens as an educative influence. He believed that education should be accompanied by a spirit of informality and joy. From the kindergarten this happy spirit began to enter and permeate the entire elementary school.

Froebel envisioned the schools as a selective environment for the socialization of children where the ways of courtesy and helpfulness were to be learned. Creative expression was to be encouraged. The seating of children in a circle was for Froebel a symbol of unity. This pattern of seating is still in use in many classrooms, not for its symbolism but for its informality. The kindergarten now has a recognized place in the elementary school program.

Froebel respected the individuality of each child and strove to develop the potentialities to be found in the individual. In the kindergarten he used play as a vehicle for that development.

Among the activities in which the child engaged were nature study, appreciation of the beautiful, weaving, sewing, gardening, clay modeling, dramatics, construction, singing, listening to stories, and the use of material called *gifts,* such as spheres, cubes, and cylinders. The gifts range from the simple to the complex. Each builds upon the previous gift but adds some new feature. Into these gifts Froebel wove an elaborate symbolism. This symbolism was later criticized among psychologists with the result that most kindergartens abandoned the symbolism.

In 1873, the first public school kindergarten was opened in St. Louis during the administration of Superintendent William T. Harris. In the next thirty years many public school kindergartens began to replace private kindergartens. In 1913 the Division of Kindergarten Education was created in the United States Bureau of Education.

Froebel did much to lessen the formality of school routine and the almost exclusuive emphasis upon book learning. Creativity helped to lift the spirit of learning. The emphasis upon the social development of children led teachers to recognize the child and his growth as of paramount importance.

Froebel believed in building the curriculum around children's interests, as their interests are symptoms of their potentialities. Modern psychologists corroborate this emphasis upon the child's interests, needs, and abilities.

Froebel's chief books were *Education of Man, Education by Development, Pedagogics of the Kindergarten,* and *Mother Play.* These books detailed his educational theories. His chief contribution to education was the kindergarten. Modern education has modified many of his theories, but many types of educational practice today still show the influence of his theories. Not only millions of kindergarten children but millions of elementary school children owed Froebel their thanks for wholesome happy classrooms as the spirit of the kindergarten moved upward into the other grades.

The influence upon American education of these four men— Rousseau, Pestalozzi, Herbart, and Froebel—is so interwoven, both in spirit and method into the fabric of the elementary school, that it would be almost impossible to isolate the contributions of the four. Our present emphasis upon self-realization has felt the impact of the individualistic educational aims of Rousseau and Pestalozzi. The second great objective of elementary education, the welfare of society, reflects the social emphasis of Herbart and Froebel. American education is infinitely the richer for both of these emphases.

The Rise of Public
Schools in the United States

The public school movement in our country followed closely upon the heels of the stimulating influence of Rousseau, Pestalozzi, Herbart, and Froebel. While the movement may be traced to the first public school legislation in the seventeenth century, no great change toward public education occurred until the beginning of the nineteenth century.

The unique characteristic of the American school system is that it is not a national system. Unlike the highly centralized education of most European countries, our system is decentralized and directed and controlled by fifty states and over 50,000 local school boards. This pattern of control resembles a quilt of many pieces, some bright, some dark. Boards of Education in wealthy states and school districts can provide better materials and pay higher teachers' salaries. Forward-looking school-board members are eager to introduce the best known educational methods into the schools, whereas unenlightened school-board personnel tend to hold back progress and reform in the schools. As a result, local control has worked both for and against the welfare of children. Certainly it has produced a very uneven distribution of educational privileges over the country as a whole.

Colonial schools. The first schools that existed in colonial days were private schools and a few public schools for paupers' children. The colonists in the northern section of the country undertook the same types of schools that they had known in England—the dame school (taught in homes with women as teachers), charity schools, and parochial schools. In the southern colonies, the upper class employed tutors for their children but children of the lower class were sent as apprentices to a craftsman to learn a trade.

In the colonial schools of New England, little more was taught than the 3 R's and the catechism. The earliest form of textbook was the hornbook (1450). The hornbook was a wooden paddle with a sheet of paper covered with transparent horn. On the paper were printed the vowels combined with consonants to form syllables. Several religious selections were included. When the pupil had mastered the text of the hornbook, he was promoted to a primer. *The New England Primer* was copied after simliar books in England and was religious in content.

The lessons were learned by heart and recited individually to the schoolmaster at his desk. A severe type of discipline prevailed with frequent use of the whipping post. This discipline was in keeping with the prevalent religious belief that a child was innately evil. The school furnishings were cheerless. The children were seated on rough wooden benches without backs. There were no blackboards, slates, or maps. There was no challenge to initiative or to original expression. The classroom was often more like a prison than an environment for happy children.

The first public school legislation. Massachusetts has the honor of passing the first legislation sponsoring free public schools. By the "Old Deluder Satan" Act of 1647 every town of fifty families was requested to maintain an elementary school under penalty of five pounds. The stated objective of this legislation was to prevent the Old Deluder, Satan, from accomplishing one chief project, namely, "to keep men from a knowledge of the Scriptures." In spite of this legislation, public schools were slow in developing.

Horace Mann and Henry Barnard. The development of the public school was stimulated by such public-spirited men as Horace Mann and Henry Barnard. These men served in their state legislatures before turning to education. They are remembered chiefly as champions of the cause of public education but they instituted school reforms as well.

Horace Mann was the first secretary of the Massachusetts State Board of Education. He was a staunch advocate of public schools as well as a critic of contemporary education. He called attention to the larger amounts spent for private schools as compared to public schools, to poor school buildings, inadequate training of teachers, and lack of uniformity in textbooks. One of his annual reports as secretary of the Board of Education in Massachusetts revealed that from three hundred to four hundred pupil-activated school rebellions per year resulted in the premature closing of the "jungle" schools before the end of the year. Mann urged a reform of the curriculum so that subjects of practical utility might have their proportionate time in the school's schedule, and he also favored the teaching of music and drawing. He encouraged the building of blackboards in schoolhouses and aided the introduction of school libraries. After a visit to Europe, he published his *Seventh Report* in which he praised methods and discipline that he had observed during a six months' tour of European schools. During Mann's secretaryship, three normal schools for the training of teachers were established. The school at Lexington, Massachusetts, built in 1839, was the first state normal school in the United States. Mann's influence outside the state of Massachusetts reached into the West and South and even into Latin America. In 1852 he became president of Antioch College.

Henry Barnard (1811–1900) devoted most of his long life to education. He was at various times in his life the first secretary of the state Board of Education of Connecticut, the first Commissioner of Education of Rhode Island, and the first United States Commissioner of Education (1867–1870).

During his secretaryship of the state Board of Education in Connecticut he carried on a heavy correspondence with teachers all over the state. One of the distinctive features of his term of office as Commissioner of Education in Rhode Island was the introduction of a traveling model school, which demonstrated methods of teaching.

Barnard had received many of his ideas on education while on several tours of Europe. He interpreted both Pestalozzi and Froebel for American readers through his first annual secretarial report, through a book on comparative education, and through the *American Journal of Education,* which he edited. From 1858 to 1860 he served as president of the University of Wisconsin, and in 1866 he became president of St. John's College in Maryland.

The struggle for public schools. The fight for public education was long and bitter. Several obstacles stood in the way of free, nonsectarian public schools. First came the idea that free education should be for paupers only. Most states had a rate system whereby parents paid a tuition fee based upon the number of children that went to school. Parents who could not afford the tuition fee had first to declare themselves paupers in order to get schooling for their children.

A second deterrent to the establishment of public schools was the idea on the part of some that the schools should teach sectarianism. At the time of the Revolutionary War, nine states had a state church and it was not until 1833 that the last state brought about disestablishment.

The forces of humanitarianism and democracy won the battle for public education in the United States. The laboring classes and middle-class liberals worked for the establishment of public schools. The chief argument in favor of public schools was that education in a democratic state was needed to induct the foreigner into the American way and to produce worthy citizens for the democratic state.

The eighteenth century produced many local school districts. As the population grew and people moved westward, homesteads were farther and farther apart. Transportation was poor and quick communication non-existent. Consequently, widely scattered district schools with local control were the rule in the West.

The Constitution of the United States did not mention education, but later the Tenth Amendment put education under control of the states. Seven of the state constitutions made provisions for the establishment of schools in the eighteenth century and other states did the same in the nineteenth century.

In order to achieve a better quality of education, the nineteenth century saw a movement toward county, city, and state control. Smaller units of education operated under the direction of the state, which distributed state funds to the local units. The states passed laws that compelled local districts to tax themselves for schools as well. The task for the twentieth century is to provide nation-wide aid for schools so as to give more equal opportunities to children, no matter in what state they happen to live.

Those who opposed the public school idea were wealthy taxpayers, persons with no children, those who believed that children of the working class were incapable of profiting from an education, private schools, and conservative religious groups who believed that a secular school would be a "godless" school.

The Lancastrian schools and the infant schools. Two existing forms of schools favored the rise of the public schools, *the Lancastrian (or monitorial) schools and the infant schools.* In 1805 the Lancastrian system was introduced into New York schools and soon spread from New England to Georgia. An almost military form of organization was practiced. At words of command, pupils rose, marched, wheeled, and opened books. An elaborate system of rewards and punishments was devised, including the dunce cap and badges of merit. The whipping post was abolished in these schools. The chief advantage of the system was obviously its economy of operation. The cost per pupil was low. The method of instruction was that of memorization. Preparation for citizenship was not a feature of this school. Since the serious drawbacks of these monitorial schools were soon evident, the Lancastrian system disappeared from the American scene. Nevertheless the system paved the way for the spread of public schools by persuading the electorate that public schools could be operated and supported by the public.

Another experiment in elementary school methods that aided the establishment of the public school was the infant school. The infant school was founded in Lanark, Scotland where Robert Owen, a British socialist, organized infant schools for children working in factories. Instead of the 3 R's, children were taught games and such ideals as cleanliness and cooperation. In England the curriculum of the infant schools was expanded to include reading, writing, and arithmetic.

In the United States the infant school idea was copied in several large cities. The success of these schools led to their incorporation into the newly formed public schools.

The graded public schools. With a rapidly increasing number of children in attendance at the free, compulsory public schools, the one-room rural school with a single teacher for children of all ages was no longer adequate. Another change that occurred at about the same time, the introduction of many subjects into the curriculum, made difficult the teaching of many grades by one teacher.

The Little Red School House was replaced in some school districts by a primary school for grades one, two, and three, and by a grammar school for grades five, six, seven, and eight. By 1900 these separate primary and grammar schools were reunited into an elementary school of eight grades. Typically, each grade was taught by a different teacher, and pupils were assigned to grades according to their age levels. Special schools were established for the blind, the deaf, and the mentally deficient children.

After a time, pupils had to master the curriculum of their grade level before they could be promoted to the next higher grade. Most schools used annual promotion plans to reclassify pupils according to their progress in the curriculum. Under the plan of annual promotion, a child who failed to meet grade standards was required to repeat a full year's work. In most city systems a plan was devised that divided the school year into two semesters so that non-promotion would mean the repetition of the work of only one-half a year.

In rural schools annual promotions remained the rule. Failure at the end of the year might be caused by lack of progress in several subjects or only in one; the child would still be required to repeat all subjects.

Today both age grouping and progress grouping are used as bases for classification of pupils into grades. There are indications, however, that the schools are moving in the direction of ungraded elementary schools.

The Traditional School

Two main types of elementary schools exist in the United States today, whether the schools be public or private. They are the traditional schools and the progressive schools. They differ in sociological bases, psychological bases, philosophical bases, discipline, and teaching-learning procedures.

Sociological bases of the traditional school. When our schools were founded, our country was a virgin land, rich in hardwood forests, mineral resources, and arable land. The population was a rural one and remained predominantly such until 1880. The principal educational institution in pioneer days was the family. Here the children, as apprentices, learned the elements of education "at the mother's knee." On the farm they learned how to plant and harvest the crops, how to care for animals, how to use tools and farm machinery.

During the slack winter months when their labor was not needed on the farm, the young went to school. Much formal schooling was considered unnecessary.

Psychological bases of the traditional school. The psychology of the traditional school was mechanistic. It attempted to explain learning in terms of what was happening in the physiological organism. This explanation is sometimes called the S-O-R theory (stimulus-organism-response), the bond theory, and connectionism.

To the connectionist the learning process was an additive one. One's total learning consisted of bond plus bond plus bond.

The chief exponent of connectionism was Edward Thorndike. His *Laws of Learning* stressed the value of learning by repeated performance, of distributive practice, of praise rather than blame, of vividness, of polarity, and of belongingness. Some of these laws are still considered valid; others have undergone change. Upon the theory of connectionism and its accompanying laws, the traditional school based its emphasis upon drill and its system of rewards and punishments.

Philosophical bases of the traditional school. Traditionalism represents a philosophy of life called *idealism* which affirms that the ultimate reality is spiritual or ideal. To develop the individual as a finite personality, the educational method should include the presentation of knowledge, the development of skills, and an ability to reason that will lead to responsible citizenship.

In the philosophy of the traditional school, cultures and their institutions were considered to be relatively stable and fixed. Education was preparation for adult life. Children were to be taught to adjust to the environment. All activity took place within the four walls of the school; the community as a resource for study or for experiencing was entirely disregarded. Some subjects, such as mathematics and grammar, were introduced for their supposed disciplinary values.

The child's mind was considered a blank tablet upon which the teacher could write at will. Therefore, the content of knowledge became of first importance. The sequence of subject matter was logical, not psychological. This resulted in much learning that had no meaning to the child. Since the program was teacher-dominated, the child had little or no opportunity to plan or explore.

The organization of the traditional school. Instruction within the classroom of the traditional school was typically directed to the group as a whole. Children were taught the same lesson at the same time. In the early schools children often sat on benches; later they were seated in rows with desks screwed to the floor.

Lessons were assigned as so many pages to be read in a textbook. Slow-learning children could not keep pace with fast-learning children, and the latter were not challenged to work up to their full potentialities.

In our first schools the basic tools of learning, the so-called 3 R's, were taught. The method used was largely drill to "stamp in" the learning. Memorization of many facts took place, but no opportunity was provided for children to solve problems or to think through to consequences. Subject matter was taught in logical order with the result that much of the learning was meaningless to the children. The various subjects were taught in short blocks of time and on a rigid time schedule. Each subject was taught independently of every other.

Discipline in the traditional school. The traditional school had as one of its purposes the development of good citizenship. Character formation, according to the traditionalists, resulted partly from example furnished by the elders and partly upon attitudes learned through precept.

The teacher provided little opportunity for guidance of pupils in inter-personal activities because there were few such activities. The school was considered a place for individual study and recitation.

Once established in the schools, authoritarian practices were slow to change, but the old order had to give place to the new because authoritarianism was in conflict with the still more firmly entrenched ideals of democracy in our political and social life.

The Transition from
Traditional to Progressive Education

In the period of educational history following the War Between the States, universal compulsory education brought changes in the public schools in organization, curriculum, and methods. Because of hesitancy to adopt the new methods, the rate of progress differed in various sections of the United States. In the industrialized cities of the Northeast, progress was rapid. The South was poverty-stricken following the War Between the States, and the task of financing schools for both the Whites and the Negroes was overwhelming. In the West schools changed rapidly from frontier schools at mid-century to modern schools at the end of the nineties, especially in cities of the far West.

The first graded elementary school in the United States was established at Quincy Grammar School in Boston in 1848. Although many other urban centers of the Northeast followed the same pattern, the country as a whole was still rural throughout most of the nineteenth century and in the rural areas, the one-room schools prevailed. In the last quarter of the nineteenth century, several states abolished the district system of education. In the Northeastern states, the district system generally gave way to the town system. A definite trend toward state certification of teachers began to show itself.

With the coming of compulsory education, the problems were many. With a heavier school population, it was at first difficult to do other than provide more of the same kind of traditional education without instituting any reforms. But changes did come in organization, curriculum, and methods before the end of the nineteenth century.

Changes in organization, curriculum, and methods. With compulsory education, it soon became obvious that all children could not be educated in the same classroom or even in the same school. The slow-learning child remained in the classroom but could not learn as fast as the bright or normal child. The size of the classes usually made individual instruction impossible with the result that the slow-learner was often left far behind the class. The schools soon learned that one curriculum could not care for the needs of all the children.

The number of subjects in the school program began to expand to meet the purposes of the newly created public schools, whose primary aim was the preparation of worthy citizens who would make the republic strong. Church control of schools was replaced by state control. Courses of studies were selected for their disciplinary value. Classicists argued that Latin and Greek were difficult subjects that would provide mental discipline for pupils. Advocates of science instruction claimed the same disciplinary value for their subjects.

In the elementary school emphasis was centered upon practical utility and moral values. Following the publication of Spencer's *What Knowledge Is of Most Worth* and Charles Darwin's *Origin of the Species,* science became a subject in the curriculum. Study of nature was the rule in the primary grades and elementary physical science in the intermediate grades. Arithmetic was a foundation for the teaching of science, and a thorough revision of arithmetic courses in the elementary school took place. A strong feeling of nationalism influenced the inclusion in the curriculum of history, geography, and civics. Grammar, literature, domestic science, and manual learning were also added. The expressive subjects such as music, art, and gymnastics found a new emphasis. Courses in bookkeeping, carpentry, current events, and agriculture were included in the schedule. An overcrowding of the curriculum resulted. With ten to twenty subjects daily, recitation of a different subject occurred every ten to twenty minutes. Multiplicity of subjects was the most prominent characteristic of curriculum development in the last half of the century.

Reforms in method to meet the purposes of a democratic state came very slowly. In a few schools the ideas of Rousseau, Pestalozzi, Herbart, and Froebel had brought innovations, but the full impact of the European influence was not felt until the twentieth century. In general, drill and the formal recitation continued their stranglehold upon the schools. An emphasis upon adult needs was reflected in the schools by spelling lists derived from adult usage and arithmetic problems most needed by adults. Little concern was shown for immediate needs of children. Changes in school method were forced through developments in psychology, sociology, and philosophy—developments that will be discussed under the heading *Progressive Education.*

Advances in scientific knowledge. The transition from traditional schools to a new education was greatly aided by developments in the world of science, by the measurement movement, which made possible a scientific evaluation of one method as compared with another, by the research studies in child growth and development, and by the work of experimental schools in widely separated sections of the United States.

Since the middle of the nineteenth century great advances in the biological, psychological, and sociological sciences began to emancipate children from teachings and disciplines founded upon less enlightened data. The findings of Francis Galton and Charles Darwin helped dispel ideas of original sin and brought about better attitudes toward children. Herbert Spencer through his book *What Knowledge Is of Most Worth?* aided the introduction of science as an important subject in the schools. The great purpose of education, he wrote, must answer the question of *how to live.* Science, he believed, had great meaning in achieving this purpose by teaching the meaning of things. Spencer urged that the teaching be made interesting and pleasurable to the learner. Through Spencer's influence, the laboratory method of teaching science was to gain wide acceptance in the public schools. Spencer asked the question as to what knowledge was needed in the lives of each person for survival and the welfare of society. Essential to living were such activities as rearing a family, earning a living, participating in political and social life, and enjoying leisure time. The business of education should fit children for these activities. These utilitarian objectives closely resemble those of the *Cardinal Principles of Secondary Education: home membership, vocational competence, worthy use of leisure time,* and *citizenship.* Similar objectives still appear in many modern curricula.

Spencer's utilitarian philosophy was applied as a minimal essentials program to fit children for adult life. Later, the child study movement and the changing conditions of our industrial and social life brought the essentialists into conflict with the ideas of progressive education, which emphasized meeting the present needs of children and providing democratic classroom living in order to improve human relations in the world.

The measurement movement. The first laboratory in experimental psychology was established in Germany in 1897 by William Wundt. Several American students worked with Wundt on the methods of the objective study of human behavior. One of these students was J. McKean Cattell (1860–1944), the first person in America to attempt the measurement of human capacity. In 1888 Cattell established an experimental laboratory at the University of Pennsylvania and in 1891 at Columbia University. In a published article, he introduced the term *mental tests.* The mental tests were first used with students at Columbia University.

Thorndike continued the work on mental tests begun by Cattell. In 1905 the Binet-Simon tests, which established norms of growth for each age, appeared in France. In 1908 Binet revised this scale and incorporated the mental-level concept. Three to eight items represented each age level from three to thirteen years. In America translations of the scale were made by Goddard, Kuhlmann, Terman and Childs. Other men, Kuhlmann (1912), Stern (1914), Yerkes, Bridges, and Hardwick suggested dividing the achievement score by the chronological age to obtain a mental quotient. In 1910 Terman used the formula $MA/CA = I.Q.$ (mental age divided by chronological age equals Intelligence Quotient). This I.Q. was multiplied by one hundred to avoid decimals. Binet's last scale was published in 1911. In this scale several reading and writing tests were omitted and five items were assigned to each age group.

In 1916 Lewis M. Terman of Stanford University revised the Binet Scale for use with children in the public schools. The scale includes items for children of three years to adults. This scale became the standard scale for use in schools and clinics. A still later revision was made by Terman and Merrill in 1937 for ages two to twenty-two. A disadvantage of these tests was that they had to be administered to children individually and the process took from one to two hours. During World War I the Army Alpha test was developed as a test to be administered to groups, and following the war, group tests for the schools were devised by Terman, Arthur S. Otis, and M. E. Haggerty. In 1919 tests called Delta I and Delta II by Haggerty were the first group tests for elementary school pupils. Despite the fact that these tests do not measure all aspects of mental ability, they do measure capacity to do school work and have been useful in classifying pupils and in predicting their scholastic capacity. Mention must also be made of the fact that intelligence tests have been sometimes misused.

The first measurement of achievement in learning paralleled the attempts at determining mental capacity. Horace Mann and S. G. Howe devised an achievement test for the Boston School examination of 1845. In 1894 J. M. Rice devised an achievement test prior to his famous study on the relationship between study time and spelling achievement. In 1903 Rice founded a Society of Educational Research. Thorndike, who had been one of Cattell's students, published the first handwriting scale in 1910. C. W. Stone in 1908 and S. A. Courtis in 1909 developed standardized achievement tests in arithmetic, and in 1913 Leonard P. Ayres, one in spelling. Many objective tests covering all subject fields flooded the market in the twenties and largely supplanted essay examinations in the schools. In best practice, teachers use objective tests to determine the retention of factual knowledge and use essays and other creative writing to give students opportunities to organize, originate, and gain facility in written expression.

Other school tests include tests of personality traits, attitude tests, special aptitudes, work habits, and study skills, but some of these are still in a developmental stage.

School surveys began to sweep the country after 1910. These surveys usually begin as self-surveys by the faculties of the schools and are followed by studies made by teams of professional educators. Entire cities and states have been surveyed and national surveys have been made as well. The methods used are comparative and the aim is to improve school practices.

Child growth and development. The child study movement had its beginnings in Europe. Rousseau urged the teacher to study his pupils. Pestalozzi kept a daily record of his own son's development and urged careful study of the progress of each individual child. Froebel studied children's interests and collected plays and nursery songs for children. Impetus was given to the child-study movement by the behaviorist school of psychology, which urged direct observation of children, and by psychoanalysts, who revealed the importance of experiences in early childhood as the cause of later adjustments or maladjustment.

A pioneer in child study in the United States was G. Stanley Hall who had studied in Germany under William Wundt. In 1880 he undertook a study of the *Contents of Children's Minds Upon Entering School.* With the assistance of four kindergarten teachers, a questionnaire of one hundred terms was given orally to determine children's understanding of common objects and some abstract terms. The results of Hall's study were published in his book *Aspects of Child Life and Education* (1907) which was translated into many foreign languages. Another work by Hall was his monumental book *Adolescence,* which was a compilation of anecdotes and facts on the physical and mental development of adolescents. These studies stimulated great interest in the study of the child.

One of these studies was that by J. M. Greenwood of Kansas City who queried first-graders and found that kindergarten children were better informed than non-kindergarten children. Several of Hall's graduate students made their own studies in child growth and development, among them Arnold Gesell, Henry H. Goddard, and Lewis M. Terman.

Gesell's experiments at Yale Institute of Human Relations were extensive studies in child development. From families of North European extraction and of middle class socio-economic status, one hundred and seven infants were selected for study. The clinic used various materials such as a cup, spoon, saucer, bell, rattle, ring, pictures, box, crayon, paper, and a ball. The reactions of the infants to these materials were recorded and filmed. Then norms were found for the performance of each age group to the materials. A child of a certain age could not manipulate the crayon and paper except to sweep it aside. The same thing occurred with learning to move forward to reach a ball. Thus a "critical" age was determined for each type of material. The critical age is the age at which an item is successfully performed by fifty per cent of the group. In this manner Gesell arrived at typical behavior for key ages. Charts were made that showed both temporary and persistent patterns.

When older children were studied, normal behavior was recorded under the headings of motor development, adaptive behavior, language development, and social development. As with the study of infants, maturity-level ratings were recorded. Marked deviations such as a fine sense of humor, originality, expressive reference to other persons, and other traits were described. These biographical records of traits make interesting and profitable reading for teachers who wish to keep anecdotal records or make reports in terms of child growth.

Gesell came to the conclusion that children passed through certain stages of development with some characteristics that were later shed as new characteristics appeared. He also emphasized the distinct individuality of each child. Other research studies by other experimenters showed that expectations as to a child's characteristics would vary for different social classes and different environments.

Gesell used co-twin studies to show the effect of environment on intelligence. In the small number of cases that he studied, he came to the conclusion that original similarities are little changed by training.

Child study associations were formed in several states and by the National Education Association. The end result was a better understanding of the individual and the widespread recognition that efficient teaching cannot be secured by knowledge of subject matter only, but must take into consideration child needs and interests.

Several universities, notably Yale, Iowa, Minnesota, Chicago, Michigan, and Harvard, have carried on scientific investigations regarding the development of the child. Findings in these centers have proved of great value in the development of sound educational practices.

Iowa studies on the relationship between I.Q. and the environment shook a prevalent belief in the constancy of the I.Q. They showed a possible closer relationship between environment and intelligence than had previously been considered possible. More recent studies at the University of Iowa have been made on group leadership and the effect of various types of social relationships upon the behavior of children, in which it was found that the democratic social climate produced the best type of behavior.

Harvard University has a Center for Research in Child Health and Development. This research has been on longitudinal studies of child health and its relationship to human development.

The new approach to child growth and development was a shift from studies of norms of behavior based upon averages of weight, height, and other measurements. Cross-sectional statistics had been found to be inadequate in the prediction of individual development. Norms have a value in showing growth tendencies within groups, but longitudinal studies compare a child with himself at different periods of development in terms of his own growth standards.

Eventually the classroom teacher began to apply the techniques of the child-study movement. Today many rating scales are used—teacher-rating scales, pupil-self-appraisal scales, interest inventories, self-expressive activities, anecdotal recordings, sociometric techniques, interviews, and case studies. These child-study techniques mark a decided step forward.

Experimental schools. Schools that pioneered in practices that differed from the traditional methods were called experimental schools. Some of these experimental practices lived for a short time , and died; others persisted. Innovations occurred in both private and public schools in different sections of the United States. Some of these experiments represented marked changes, others only slight differences from the traditional method. Many individuals in widely separated sections of the United States helped bring about a reform movement that eventually swept the country so that it was felt in almost every school. The majority of schools were slow in attempting extreme changes; a few schools are still unaffected by the reforms in education.

The Quincy schools. The possibility of scientifically measuring the educational product proved of considerable aid to schools that wished to try experimental procedures. One of the early experiments was at Quincy, Massachusetts under the superintendency of Francis W. Parker. Instead of the usual separate subjects, Parker introduced a correlation of subject matter. Arts and crafts were part of the correlated program. Parents charged that the Quincy schools had been turned into mud-pie factories. But when the Massachusetts State Board of Education conducted an examination in the 3 R's and such content subjects as history and geography, the Quincy students surpassed other students in basic skills and knowledge. Parker had spent several years of study in Europe and was familiar with the practices of Pestalozzi and Froebel. When he became an administrator of the Quincy schools, he abolished the separate teaching of reading, arithmetic, history, and geography and taught these subjects as parts of an interrelated unit. Learning became a cooperative community enterprise, not a system of granting rewards and wielding threats and punishments. Slow-learning pupils received extra coaching in their school work. A spirit of activity and delightful cheerfulness was reported by visitors to the Quincy schools. Parker's influence upon education was further extended when he took over the leadership of the Cook County Normal School. Its laboratory school was made into a community school. Field trips, nature study, and industrial arts were featured.

The John Dewey Laboratory School. The University of Chicago Laboratory School was called The John Dewey School. It was operated by John Dewey and his wife Alice Chapman Dewey from 1896 to 1904. Work tables took the place of the individual desks usually found in classrooms. The school demonstrated Dewey's belief that intellectual growth grew best out of action arising from problem-solving situations. Dewey's practical experience in this school helped round out the pragmatic philosophy on which he later wrote extensively.

Other early laboratory schools were the Cook County Normal School, the Horace Mann School, the Speyer School, and the Lincoln School of Teachers College, Columbia University.

An industrial arts school. The Workingman's School in New York, later called The Ethical Culture School, had Felix Adler (1851–1933) as its director. He introduced work activities into the schools. He advocated replacing object-teaching with object-creating. Training of both the hand and the brain was the objective. Four hours of constructive work, and two hours of drawing per week were scheduled for each grade of the elementary school. Other schools in the United States were stimulated to undertake similar activities.

Contract plans. The Dalton, Massachusetts Plan was an experiment to eliminate short assignments and give children an opportunity to concentrate upon their work over longer periods of time and at varying rates of speed. The plan was instituted by Helen Parkhurst, who was greatly influenced by the ideas of Marie Montessori. Montessori has been called the John Dewey of European schools, so great was her impact upon elementary schools in Europe. Helen Parkhurst introduced a contract plan whereby the pupils agreed to finish a given piece of work in a specified length of time, usually a month. A laboratory was provided where pupils had a wide variety of materials to explore. This plan allowed the pupil much freedom. Daily sessions helped pupils to plan and receive guidance. The Dalton Plan did not spread widely in the United States, but was copied more extensively in England and, for a short length of time, in Russia. The contract plan as it originated in Dalton has been discontinued as a major method.

Scarsdale, New York used the contract plan for a single day's work. Other schools used a plan-for-a-day without labeling the method a contract. In these schools, teachers and pupils planned together the day's activities. Except for scheduled group projects, the pupils could then proceed at individual rates of speed, and those who finished early could pursue activities or studies of their own interests.

Contracts for school study were often on three levels, such as X, Y, and Z levels. Each level varied in degrees of difficulty. The Z level contained the minimum essentials of the school project and had to be completed before the X and Y levels were started. This procedure enabled fast learners to move ahead until all three contracts were completed. One criticism made of these contract plans was the lack of creative activities at the lowest level, so that the slow learner was reduced to routine practices without the spur of inventive endeavors.

Plans for individual instruction. Three experiments in individual instruction were the Pueblo Plan, the St. Louis Plan, and the Winnetka Plan. The Pueblo Plan was developed in Pueblo, Colorado where Preston W. Search (1853–1932) was Superintendent of Public Schools. This plan permitted individual progress and promotion at any time of the school year that the work of the grade was completed. Each pupil in the Pueblo schools worked by himself at his own rate of speed, except in such group work as physical education and music. In 1901 Search published statistics on individual growth and differences in school abilities and performance. He also published an age-grade table that called attention to retardation in the schools.

The St. Louis Plan was directed by William T. Harris, who is also remembered for the introduction of the first American kindergarten into his schools. His plan differed from the usual annual or half-annual promotions. He tried to meet individual differences by a frequent shifting of pupils into classes that would meet their immediate needs. He describes the plan as follows:

In St. Louis there is no attempt to bring all classes within the same grade to one standard of advancement, so that, e.g., in January, all pupils within a given grade shall have arrived at just the same point in a study. At all times there are new classes just beginning the work of a grade, or year's work, in some one of our schools. The classes are not separated by intervals of one year in their work, but by irregular intervals varying from six weeks to twenty. It is considered desirable to have these intervals small, so that reclassification may be more easily managed. Pupils who fall behind their class for any reason (such as absence, lack of physical strength or of mental ability) may be reclassified with the next lower class without falling back a year, and thereby becoming discouraged. Pupils who are unusually bright or mature, may be promoted to the class above, or form new classes with the slower pupils of the class above, who need to review their work. . . . The disturbance in classes is very slight, compared with the advantages gained by the teacher in being relieved of the necessity to drive the laggards, and drill and cram them to make them keep up with the average of the class. The teacher was once obliged to spend most of her time upon the dull ones in the useless endeavor to force them to make up lost time, or to equal the strides of the more mature, more regular, or more brilliantly gifted pupils, and, of course, these latter pupils lost proportionately, and the net result of the process was to overwork the incompetent, and to hold back the competent ones. The teacher, in the vain effort to hold together the extremes of her class, separating more widely every day till the end of the year, became cross and petulant, and sank continually into the abyss of drill-machine pedagogy.[6]

The Winnetka, Illinois Plan, undertaken by Carleton Washburne in 1919, became widely known for its individualization of instruction, but group activities were also included in the daily program. In the experiment, spelling and reading were the first subjects learned by pupils at individual rates of speed, and later other subjects such as arithmetic, geography, history, and language were added to the list. Teachers who were subject-matter experts were available in various rooms called laboratories to give help as needed. Each pupil proceeded at his own rate of speed. To illustrate, a pupil might complete a year's curriculum in arithmetic in six months, his spelling in a year, but another subject might take him more than a year. Half of the school day was devoted to such group activities as music, art, games, dramatics, and shop.

---

[6] William T. Harris, "Annual Report of the Superintendent," *Twenty-First Annual Report of the Board of Directors of the St. Louis Public Schools* (St. Louis, Missouri, August 1, 1875), pp. 28–29.

The precise details of the Winnetka Plan did not spread widely to other public schools, but individual instruction in some form or other is a cherished quality of education in modern classrooms.

Assistant-teacher plan. Batavia, New York experimented with two teachers per room, one teacher to conduct classes and an assistant teacher to aid the slow learners. More pupils per room were possible under this plan. The bright pupils received no individual attention. One fallacy of the plan was the belief that slow learners could be brought up to grade standards by more attention, even when they did not have the mental ability to do so.

The platoon school. The Gary, Indiana schools launched the Platoon School under the superintendency of William Wirt. The platoon idea involved the multiple use of classrooms. Two groups of pupils (called platoons) used the same classrooms alternately. School hours ran from 8:30 A.M. to 5:00 P.M.

The greatly increased enrollment in our schools following World War II has forced many schools into multiple use of classrooms with double sessions, in a manner not dissimilar to the platoon schools.

Action research. The Hills School, Huntington, Long Island carried on a two-year action research program in creative writing in the 1930's under the principalship of Lawrence MacNiece. Children from grades three through eight in matched groups were involved in the project, as was the entire faculty. The results showed the value of rich stimulating experiences for the development of imaginative expression. Excursions by school bus were made to farms, gardens, cathedrals, science and art museums, and industries.[7]

Improvement of classroom teaching. A realization on the part of many teachers that the routine of assign-study-recite on the 3 R's made a dreary school day led to improvements in many classrooms. First of all came the introduction of new subject matter in addition to the tool subjects of reading, spelling, and arithmetic. Also children began to read for a purpose—to enjoy literature, to explore nature, and to identify with history. They learned to spell in order to write. Arithmetic became more functional as many impractical problems were omitted from textbooks.

Change in methods of teaching came more gradually. Some teachers varied the question-and-answer method with reports on

7 Ruby Warner, "Creative Writing Through Creative Teaching" (Doctor's Thesis, New York University, 1942).

assigned topics or on subjects chosen voluntarily. Discussion of community problems gave more opportunity for pupil expression. Extra-curricular activities such as dramatics, sewing, or art clubs were formed in order to appeal to individual interests.

Then came the activity schools in which children engaged in some project as part of the daily program. Pupils who formerly had to raise their hands for permission to leave their seats were allowed to move more freely about the room when they were engaged in construction such as building a post office, an Indian tepee, or an airplane.

The modern philosophy of progressive education ushered in the child-centered schools in opposition to book-centered schools. Later the community schools with their social emphasis retained the emphasis on the child as learner but added to the curriculum some of the problems of society with which children as future citizens needed to be aware.

A growing realization of the necessity of studying and analyzing individual children was increasingly evident in classroom practice. Common observation revealed the boredom of those gifted children who were compelled to move at a pace too slow for their bright mentality and frustration of the dull pupils for whom lessons moved too fast. As a result of these inequalities in ability, disciplinary problems arose as pupils rebelled against the restrictions of the classroom.

Progressive Education

What is progressive education? Progressive education means many things to different people. Some persons judge progressive schools from a few early schools that went to extremes in their revolt against the disadvantages of the old techniques. These schools, in their focus upon the interests, abilities, and needs of children, reportedly were so child-centered that they failed in their social objectives. A few schools, in permitting more freedom of action to children, were lax in guiding them toward responsibility.

The progressive school is one that is constantly trying to move forward in improved methods of teaching and learning that apply the best findings of research in sociology, psychology, and philosophy.

Sociological bases of progressive education. In the twentieth century the population is no longer rural; we are an urban civilization. Work that previously went on in the home moved to the factory. Many women became wage earners. Children no longer learned "at the mother's knee"; the family as an educational institution was weakened. A greater burden of teaching fell upon the schools. The school that had been teaching the 3 R's almost exclusively now had to teach behavioral controls, the chief values of our democratic culture, and additional subject matter.

Although the status of women was raised as a result of the industrial revolution and the participation of women in work outside the home, more of the marriages now ended in divorce. Many children failed to find affection and security in the home. A great wave of juvenile delinquency broke over the country. The school had to change its rigid discipline and competitive ways in order to provide security and feelings of worth and achievement for all children.

On the national and international level our age has been one of alternating periods of prosperity and depressions, of wars and revolutions, of anxieties and unrest. All of these socio-economic conditions are reflected in the schools with an increased emphasis upon the social studies and upon human relations in all the aspects of school life.

Psychological bases of progressive education. Modern education is based upon organismic psychology which considers the organism acting as a whole. Hence the modern dictum: We teach the *whole* child. The teacher considers not only the mental reactions of the child but his physical and emotional reactions as well. Subjects are no longer taught separately but are fused in order that relationships may be seen and insights gained. A country is not studied apart from its neighbors. Mathematical concepts are first considered as wholes before being analyzed into their parts. Beginning reading instruction focuses upon seeing words as wholes, not as separate letters. Work is undertaken by pupils to seek the solution to a problem, and not to gain rewards or prizes. Organismic psychology proclaims the whole as greater than the sum of its parts and as being more than the sum of its parts. It emphasizes the gestalt theory of experiencing: configuration, form, and patterns. Instead of merely memorizing lessons, the pupil, in a spirit of inquiry, makes discoveries for himself. He is an active agent in purposing, experiencing, and evaluating. The new psychology suggests that the school focus upon the growth of the child in the ways most prized by our society.

Philosophical bases of progressive education. As the twentieth century advanced, a new philosophy of education began to permeate almost every elementary school. In places where it is not accepted in whole, it is being practiced in part. The chief exponent of the new philosophy was John Dewey.

John Dewey (1859–1952). John Dewey, one of the greatest philosophers of our time, was born in Burlington, Vermont in 1859. He was graduated from the University of Vermont in 1879 and received his Ph.D at Johns Hopkins in 1884. He taught at the following universities: Minnesota (1888–89), Michigan (1889–94), Chicago (1894–1904), and Columbia (1904–30). While serving as Director of the School of Education at the University of Chicago, he had the opportunity of putting into practice his educational ideas in the laboratory school there. The John Dewey School of the University of Chicago was the first experimental school in the United States.

The influence of Dewey's philosophy spread not only in the United States but in many foreign lands. He lectured at the University of Peking and aided the Turkish government in the reorganization of its national schools.

Dewey's philosophy owes much to the individualism of Rousseau and Pestalozzi and to the social emphasis of Froebel. In Dewey, the ideas of these earlier educational reformers came to fuller fruition. Dewey, moreover, went a step further than any of these men in his concept that the pupil must participate, as part of his school experiences, as a contributing member of society. An effective school, he said, cannot exist in isolation from the community.

Possibly no other philosophy has been more misunderstood than that of John Dewey, both by his followers and by his critics. Some of his followers picked up his concise and pungent sayings and used them as slogans for school practices that Dewey himself would have been the first to criticize. Many of his critics show an honest disagreement with his ideas while others display by their remarks their complete misunderstanding. Since the advent of Sputnik, he has been blamed for all the faults of the American schools, for juvenile delinquency, as well as for our failure to put a satellite into orbit ahead of the Russians.

Dewey's philosophy is that of instrumentalism, a philosophy which holds that the various forms of human activity are instruments developed by man to solve his problems. Instrumentalism bears a close resemblance to pragmatism, which states that truth is measured by experimental results and practical outcomes that can be shared and tested by all who investigate. It insists upon the need for constant verification of hypotheses. The principles of pragmatism were introduced as a formal discipline by C. S. Peirce (1898). To John Dewey goes the credit of working out the instrumentalist aspects of the pragmatic doctrine.

Like other great writers, Dewey had the power of putting much into few words. In this manner he sought to call attention to urgent needs in our educational system. Some of the chief tenets of his philosophy are expressed in these pithy phrases. Several of these ideas will be discussed briefly:

1. *We learn to do by doing.* Modes of behavior are best learned by actual performance. We become moral by being moral. Dewey called attention to the fact that the traditional school taught chiefly through books, not through direct experiencing. Before formal instruction begins, children are educated by participation in actual situations, and all through life one's own experiences mean more than those which are learned vicariously.

2. *Education is life, not preparation for life.* Here again Dewey points out one of the evils of existing school practice, which was so intent upon preparing children for adult life that it failed to take into consideration what was happening to the welfare of the child as he learned. Dewey's idea was that life in the classroom should be worth living in its own right, and that a good present life is the best preparation for the future. This tenet of his philosophy has also been interpreted to mean that all of life from birth to death, in and out of school, is a continuous education.

3. *Education is growth.* A corollary of this principle is that interest is an indication of growth. The task of the school becomes one of providing interests on increasingly mature levels that meet the needs of growing children. As children attempt to solve the problems that arise out of their interests, they make hypotheses as to possible solutions, gather and sift pertinent knowledge, and arrive at tentative solutions. Thus they learn to think. Learning to think becomes a method of instruction. The thinking of the children gives rise to new interests. Education becomes growth.

4. *The school is primarily a social institution.* To Dewey, democracy was a primary ethical concept. He declared that the schools must be democratic if democracy is to be more than a political machine. His influence on behalf of democracy did much to abolish authoritarian practices in the schools. Dewey maintained that the school must be an organized form of democratic living; a democratic culture could not be achieved unless the schools were a reflection of that environment. Therefore, the discipline of the school should proceed not from one person alone but from the life of the school as a whole. Dewey believed that the child becomes conscious of his culture by performing the fundamental types of activity of that culture. He did not favor the individual at the expense of society, though he believed that the starting point of education was the child's own powers. Education must meet the child's felt needs and interests. The traditional school had emphasized academic learning but neglected concomitant learnings such as the physical and emotional reactions of children.

In *Democracy and Education* Dewey wrote:

> Learning is the accompaniment of continuous activities or occupations which have a social aim and utilize the materials of typical social situations. For under such conditions the school becomes itself a form of social life . . . All education which develops power to share effectively in social life is moral. It forms a character which not only does the particular socially necessary but one which is interested in the continuous readjustment which is essential to growth. Interest in learning from all the contacts of life is the essential moral-interest.[8]

By sharing in the government of the school, the child will realize his position as a contributing member of the school society. Social efficiency results from participation in social institutions. Outcomes will be more successful when purposive planning has been part of the experience. Children will then learn to set new and increasingly higher levels of purposing. The school should provide a simple and selective environment in which the child can experience as many of the activities as our culture considers to be worthy. The school becomes a miniature social community in which unworthy features of the outside world are eliminated.

The desirable society is one which permits participation in its

---

[8] John Dewey, *Democracy and Education* (New York: The Macmillan Company, 1938), p. 418. With permission.

benefits for all its members on equal terms. Such a society must have an education that gives individuals a personal interest in social relationships and habits of mind which secure social changes without disorder. An undesirable society, on the other hand, is one which sets up barriers to free communication of experience. Dewey's philosophy had a great impact upon our schools because it interpreted and harmonized with the demands of our democratic nation.

5. *The center of correlation is the child's own social activities.* In fairly recent educational literature, there have appeared such terms as correlation, integration, and the core curriculum. What shall be the core? History, geography, and literature as Herbart suggested? Or shall it be mathematics and science? Or English? Dewey would have as the center of the curriculum the child's own social activities.

As to method, Dewey is never prescriptive. This would be too limiting for the teacher. The creative teacher has succeeded in the progressive method. Pupils in turn have become more skillful in planning their activities and more alert in finding inventive ways of solving problems.

Among John Dewey's writings are *My Pedagogic Creed* (1897), *Democracy and Education* (1916), *Reconstruction in Philosophy* (1920) and *Art as Experience* (1934).

An educational classic that embodies the essence of John Dewey's philosophy is *My Pedagogic Creed*. Excerpts from this writing are quoted so as to give the reader the philosopher's own words:

> *Article One—What Education Is.* I Believe that . . . all education proceeds by the participation of the individual in the social consciousness of the race. This process begins unconsciously almost at birth, and is continually shaping the individual's powers, saturating his consciousness, forming his habits, training his ideas, and arousing his feelings and emotions. Thru this unconscious education the individual gradually comes to share in the intellectual and moral resources which humanity has succeeded in getting together. He becomes an inheritor of the funded capital of civilization. The most formal and technical education in the world cannot safely depart from this general process. It can only organize it or differentiate it in some particular direction.
>
> . . . the only true education comes thru the stimulation of the child's powers by the demands of the social situations in which he finds himself. Thru these demands he is stimulated to act as a member of a unity, to emerge from his original narrowness of action and feeling, and to conceive of himself from the standpoint of the wel-

fare of the group to which he belongs. Thru the responses which others make to his own activities he comes to know what these mean in social terms.

. . . In sum, I believe that the individual who is to be educated is a social individual, and that society is an organic union of individuals. If we eliminate the social factor from the child we are left only with an abstraction; if we eliminate the individual factor from society, we are left only with an inert and lifeless mass. Education, therefore, must begin with a psychological insight into the child's capacities, interests, and habits. It must be controlled at every point by reference to these same considerations. These powers, interests, and habits must be continually interpreted—we must know what they mean. They must be translated into terms of their social equivalents—into terms of what they are capable of in the way of social service.

Article Two—What the School Is. I Believe that . . . the school is primarily a social institution. Education being a social process, the school is simply that form of community life in which all those agencies are concentrated that will be most effective in bringing the child to share in the inherited resources of the race, and to use his own powers for social ends.

. . . education, therefore, is a process of living and not a preparation for future living.

. . . the school must represent present life, life as real and vital to the child as that which he carries on in the home, in the neighborhood, or on the playground.

. . . the teacher is not in the school to impose certain ideas or to form certain habits in the child, but is there as a member of the community to select the influences which shall affect the child and to assist him in properly responding to these influences.

Article Three—The Subject Matter of Education. I Believe that . . . the social life of the child is the basis of concentration or correlation, in all his training or growth. The social life gives the unconscious unity and the background of all his efforts and of all his attainments.

. . . the subject matter of the school curriculum should mark a gradual differentiation out of the primitive unconscious unity of social life.

. . . we violate the child's nature and render difficult the best ethical results by introducing the child too abruptly to a number of special studies, of reading, writing, geography, etc., out of relation to this social life.

. . . there is . . . no succession of studies in the ideal school curriculum. If education is life, all life has, from the outset, a scientific aspect, an aspect of art and culture, and an aspect of communication. It cannot, therefore, be true that the proper studies for one grade are mere reading and writing, and that at a later grade, reading, or literature, or science, may be introduced. The progress is not in the succession of studies, but in the development of new attitudes towards, and new interests in, experience.

. . . education must be conceived as a continuing reconstruction of experience; that the process and the goal of education are one and the same thing.

Article Four—The Nature of Method. I Believe that . . . the question of method is ultimately reducible to the question of the order of development of the child's powers and interests. The law for presenting and treating material is the law implicit within the child's own nature. Because this is so I believe the following statements are of supreme importance as determining the spirit in which education is carried on.

. . . the active side precedes the passive in the development of the child-nature; that expression comes before conscious impression; that the muscular development precedes the sensory; that movements come before conscious sensations; I believe that consciousness is essentially motor or impulsive; that conscious states tend to project themselves in action.

. . . the neglect of this principle is the cause of a large part of the waste of time and strength in school work. The child is thrown into a passive, receptive, or absorbing attitude. The conditions are such that he is not permitted to follow the law of his nature; the result is friction and waste.

. . . interests are the signs and symptoms of growing power. I believe that they represent dawning capacities. Accordingly the constant and careful observation of interests is of the utmost importance for the educator.

Article Five—The School and Social Progress. I Believe that . . . education is the fundamental method of social progress and reform.

. . . education is a regulation of the process of coming to share in the social consciousness; and that the adjustment of individual activity on the basis of this social consciousness is the only sure method of social reconstruction.

. . . the community's duty to education is . . . its paramount moral duty. By law and punishment, by social agitation and discussion, society can regulate and form itself in a more or less haphazard and chance way. But thru education society can formulate its own purposes, can organize its own means and resources, and thus shape itself with definiteness and economy in the direction in which it wishes to move.

. . . every teacher should realize the dignity of his calling; that he is a social servant set apart for the maintenance of proper social order and the securing of the right social growth.[9]

---

[9] John Dewey, *My Pedagogic Creed* (New York: E. L. Kellogg & Co., 1897).

A disciple and interpreter of John Dewey is William Heard Kilpatrick. From 1909 until his retirement in 1938, he taught at Teachers College, Columbia University. Dr. Kilpatrick lectured to large classes of teachers and students on the philosophy of education. He was more specific on methods than John Dewey and was one of the advocates of the project method. He thought of a project as a purposeful activity carried on and completed in a natural setting. Among his writings are *Foundations of Method, Source Book in the Philosophy of Education,* and *Education and the Social Crisis.*

CHAPTER II

Significant Trends
in Modern Education

Out of the sociological, psychological, and philosophical bases of modern education there has arisen a number of significant trends in teaching and learning practices: creative procedures, a child study movement with findings about child growth and development, a promising emphasis upon meeting the individual differences of children, the use of group dynamics, sociometric and projective techniques for understanding and adjustment of children's needs, increased use of the scientific method in teaching, a new concept of discipline, better materials of instruction, and evaluation procedures that measure achievement of the new goals of education.

Creative Education

One of the most significant trends in today's schools is the encouragement of creativity. Human advancement comes through original thought and invention. To encourage original thought and invention is the great role of creative education. To this end the modern school awakens and develops whatever is unique and distinctive in every individual child, irrespective of psychological, physical, or social-class differences. A way of excellence is encouraged in all endeavors whether of intellectual, aesthetic, or moral import. Creative education becomes a key to greatness of effort and of spirit.

More than at any time in our generation, the public today is clamoring for more creativity; science and mathematics, government, industry, and business are calling for creative minds.

When children enter school they bring with them a unique imagination. This imaginative gift may vanish if it is not cultivated. Margaret Mead, noted anthropologist, writing about the place of the school in the American culture, admonishes the school to preserve this spirit of originality into the mature years of the individual:

> From the teachers of little children we need a cheerful willingness to preserve in the child that which is there. We need not only a will-

ingness to welcome the way in which the child unites its individual phantasy with the fantasy creatures of its culture, but we also need new inventions in which the child will be left free to integrate through life with the vividness and immediacy, and concrete images so easily come by in childhood. We must devise new ways . . . of making that early awareness a continuing part of the personality into adulthood and old age. We need, in fact, to do for the many men what accidents of gift and history made possible in the occasional great geniuses of the past.[1]

Good schools foster creativity through the organization of the entire school program and some through creative expression in the arts alone.

Creativity in the general organization. Where creativity is fostered through organization of the entire school program, children help to set their own goals, plan their own activities, work in groups in which opinions can be shared, and continuously engage in evaluations that set ever higher goals of endeavor. Here creativity exists in the entire fabric. Children have the liberty to experiment, opportunity to find new ways of handling material, and freedom to express their own unique personalities. Through this creative program, children are helped to find themselves. Imitation makes dullards; originality makes participants of us all. Experience is enriched by expression; the expressive phase of activity gives meaning to experience. Creativity serves to quicken perception, strengthen emotion, and unify interests. The creative mind gives pleasure as imagination is allowed to play.

The trained teacher may ask questions that lead to inquiry and discovery. The right questions can lead to a high degree of creativity. The facts learned may be organized into conceptualizations that are new for the learners. Although facts in themselves do not produce imagination, nevertheless, imagination depends upon the facts of experience for building new ideas. The superior organization shows relationships among facts, discovers the similarities and differences among things in the universe, tests hypotheses already formulated, helps to solve problems, and keeps alive the spirit of adventure in learning.

Creative expression in the arts. In addition to creative education in the general program, many schools encourage creative expression

---

[1] Margaret Mead, *The School in American Culture* (Cambridge: Harvard University Press, 1951), pp. 38–41. With permission.

through the arts—creative writing, painting, music, crafts, rhythmic activity, and dramatics.

Experience has shown that creative expression flowers best in a warm friendly atmosphere where opportunities are provided for the gathering of abundant information and where a wide variety of expressive materials is readily available.

Creative art is the organization of experience so that new wholes appear. Imagination cannot exist in a vacuum. Creative expression follows creative teaching. The teacher provides inspiration and appreciation. The creative spirit does not thrive on criticism, and the desire for mere correctness may stifle uniqueness. This does not mean that good workmanship is not prized, but in creative expression originality and invention are the main objectives.

Schools that have encouraged the creative arts have found that the imagination of young children can often be preserved through all the years of school life. Collections of the imaginative work of children in the arts can be found in *Creative Expression* by Gertrude Hartmann[2] and Ann Shumaker, *Creative Youth* by Hughes Mearns,[3] and *The Child and His Elementary School World* by Ruby H. Warner.[4]

Child Growth and Development

Research findings about the ways in which children grow and develop help the teacher to understand children. Through the child-study movement, both vertical and lateral studies of children were made that yielded detailed information of individual children and also group characteristics at various age levels.

Principles of child growth and development. Two important findings from the child-study movement are (1) that each child is unique and (2) that each age group has certain characteristics that are typical of that group.

It is important that the child preserve his own uniqueness. The teacher who helps the child acquire and maintain a sense of his own worth is the one most likely to help him preserve his uniqueness.

[2] Gertrude Hartmann and Ann Shumaker, *Creative Expression* (New York: The John Day Company, 1932).

[3] Hughes Mearns, *Creative Youth* (New York: Doubleday & Company, Inc., 1929).

[4] Ruby H. Warner, *The Child and His Elementary School World* (Englewood Cliffs, New Jersey: Prentice-Hall, Inc., 1958), Chs. 3, 5, and 9.

Such a teacher provides an atmosphere of friendliness, a feeling of togetherness, and many opportunities for achievement.

Not only is each child unique but he has certain characteristics in common with other children of the same age level. Some of these common characteristics are typically shed as the child moves on to the next age level. For example, the child six or seven years old likes to tattle, but by eight years of age he is less likely to tell tales of others' behavior.

These growth sequences, says Arnold Gesell, are seldom or never circumvented. The knowledge of age norms of child growth and development cannot be applied arbitrarily, but they do give a teacher an understanding of a system of relationships that change with the growth of the child and a perspective that is invaluable in the guidance of children.[5]

Developmental characteristics of children at ages six and seven. Children in grades one and two engage mostly in individual activities. They are very active and can sit still for little more than ten minutes at a time. They are better able to use large muscles than small ones. Their attention span is short. They respond best to a rhythmic sequence of work, play, and rest. They are curious and imaginative. They are unaware of many things in the environment and need experiences with concrete objects. They may display contradictory social responses. They try to achieve independence but still need adult support and approval.

The sixth year is an age of transition for physical and emotional change. This child tends to go to emotional extremes. He finds it difficult to make choices. His sense of time is not well developed; for him, time is present time or his own time.

The child of seven is in somewhat better balance emotionally, but he tends to overdo in both work and play. He likes to please and is self-critical. He enjoys the personal attention of his teacher. His favorite stories are fairy tales and simple adventures in science.

Developmental characteristics of children at ages eight and nine. Children at ages eight and nine are energetic and daring. They are more group conscious than formerly and like the feeling of togetherness provided by group activities. They show more social responsibility and are willing to abide by group rules. They are relatively

---

[5] Arnold Gesell, *The Child from Five to Ten* (New York: Harper & Brothers, 1946).

free of prejudice. They will wait their turn. They are increasingly self-directive.

The eight-year-old enjoys telling tall tales. Reading of comics reaches a peak at his age. Children of eight prefer to make a choice rather than to be told directly what to do.

Nines show a growing independence of thought and action. They have strong likes and dislikes. They work hard to perfect skills. They need more opportunities for planning, reasoning, and independent action. Their sense of historical time is fairly well developed. They tend to be perfectionists.

Developmental characteristics of children at ages ten and eleven. At ten and eleven years of age, children like to play and work in groups of their own peers. They are idealistic, easily excited, and somewhat secretive. They show an interest in simple social problems. They want fair play. Participation in club activities has a special appeal, and small group activities in school satisfy the need for belonging. The approval of their peers means more to them than the commendation of adults. Hero worship is characteristic of this age. These children have a large range of interests that need to be encouraged and reinforced. They progress rapidly in their ability to form generalizations. They like to collect and arrange exhibits. They are increasingly successful with problem-solving activities.

Ten-year-olds show manual dexterity in the construction of woodwork, exhibits, and models. They like to play in large groups and enjoy organized games. Their growth is so rapid that they are easily fatigued.

At age eleven, girls are more mature than boys. When the girls are absorbed in such academic subjects as history and geography, the thoughts of the boys are likely to center upon baseball and football. Some eleven-year-olds are just leaving childhood while others are approaching adolescence.

Knowledge of the developmental characteristics of children guides the teacher in adjusting her expectations of a child's growth to the findings of behavioral development.

Uniqueness of growth. Although there is a sequence of growth for all children, the rate varies for different individuals. In other words, children can be expected to move through definite cycles of growth but no specific age can be given at which all children will show certain characteristics. Nevertheless, children of each age level tend to have similiar intellectual, physical, social, and emotional characteristics.

As individuals, children differ greatly in their native ability, in rate of maturation, and in emotional development. All children, therefore, cannot develop skills at the same time or with the same degree of success. Each pupil has his own unique pattern for learning.

The child develops in his own way as he attempts to satisfy his desires. To accomplish maximum development for the child, the teacher observes and evaluates each child's characteristics. With this knowledge she can adapt work to interests, expectations to abilities, and ambitions to talents.

Children differ in abilities, both physical and mental. We readily recognize physical differences such as those of weight and height. We also know that people differ in mental ability. The levels of general ability, according to Wechsler's I.Q. Scale, are as follows: 50 per cent of children are average (90–109 I.Q.); 16 per cent, dull (80–89); and 16 per cent, bright (110–120). About 9 per cent have superior or very superior intellects, and about the same per cent are either mentally defective or borderline.[6] All of these children may be found in the classroom with the exception of those with I.Q.'s below 70, who have been placed in special-education classes or schools. The general intelligence tests do not reveal special aptitudes such as art or music. What they do predict reasonably well is ability to succeed in academic studies.

Children differ not only in their potentialities for intellectual stature but in the environments from which they come. Whereas heredity determines how far a person can go, the environment determines how far he will go within the limits set by heredity.

Another way in which children show their uniqueness is in the number, kind, and degree of intensity of their interests. The more that is known of the individual's interests, the more effective the instructional program is likely to be.

Uniqueness is also shown in children's emotional needs and social relationships. Some children are more mature in their emotional adjustment than others. Children differ in social relationships; some are shy, others very friendly. Attitudes and ideals vary markedly

6 Sidney L. Pressey, Francis P. Robinson, and George E. Horrocks, *Psychology in Education* (New York: Harper & Brothers, 1959), pp. 61–62.

from child to child. Teaching practices used by the school to meet the varying abilities and interests of each child will be discussed in the following sections.

Meeting Individual Differences

One of the most encouraging improvements in today's schools is the attempt to meet individual differences among children in satisfying ways. These individual differences include variation in special interests and talents, physical and mental ability, emotional needs, readiness for learning, and subject-matter achievement.

Meeting individual differences in children's interests. Although children tend to follow the interests of other children of their own age level, they also show interest patterns that are highly individual. Interests are personal as well as group-directed. Wide variations are shown in the total interests of children. The ambitions of two boys, for example, may both be centered upon aviation, but Joe may spend his leisure time at mechanical pursuits while Ralph plays baseball. A further analysis of the interests of these two boys will yield quite different interest patterns.

A knowledge of the individual interests of children is a prerequisite to effective teaching. Without this knowledge, the ability of the teacher to motivate learning is difficult, if not impossible. It is through past and present interests that new desires for learning arise.

Interests involve feelings. When interests are satisfied, the child experiences an expansion of the self. When they are denied, he feels frustrated. Desires expand if they meet with approval and encouragement, and they tend to weaken if they do not bring satisfaction and a feeling of success.

To determine what children's interests may be, teachers observe children in the classroom, on the playground, and in their homes. Interests will be most readily apparent when children are free to choose their own activities. Children's conversation and written compositions reveal their needs and interests. The kind of library books and of audio-visual programs that children admire are still another source of data. A child is interested in those activities for which he has talent. Checklists of children's interests may be helpful to the teacher.

In the classroom, the teacher finds that a child's interest is a powerful urge to activity. When interest grips a child, new ideas spring up. Curiosity leads to many educational activities. A child may want to read, to figure, or to construct. One interest may lead to another, or the original interest may be strengthened by a successful pursuit.

Today's schools are recognizing the human interest people have in talking and working together. The encouragement of small-group or committee work is highly desirable from the point of view of interest.

The teacher plans the program so that children will succeed with the quest of desirable interests and receive recognition for achievement.

Meeting individual differences in physical needs. Children of a particular age differ from those of another age in physical needs. A six-year-old needs much activity. It is difficult for him to sit still for more than ten minutes. The first-grade teacher takes cognizance of this need for activity by permitting freedom of movement especially at the beginning of the school year. She alternates periods of motor activity and of rest. At this age, too, the child's larger muscles are better developed than his finer muscles, and this is one of the reasons why manuscript writing is used in the first two or three grades. The attention span is short in the first grade. In the intermediate grades, children enjoy vigorous activities that develop strength, speed, and endurance. Their attention span has increased. They can sit still for longer periods of time.

Not only do children of different ages differ in physical characteristics and needs, but children within a given age show individual differences. Some are more quiescent than others. Some are sensitive to variations from the average in such characteristics as height or weight; others take similar variations without undue concern. For some, growth may proceed so rapidly that fatigue may interfere with work.

Meeting individual differences in emotional needs. Just as the profession of medicine is beginning to adopt a preventive approach to the problems of health, so also the teaching profession is taking positive steps to forestall emotional disturbances in children. For every ill there is a cause and behind emotional ills are unmet needs of children, the most important of which is the need to be an individual of dignity and worth. Feelings of unworthiness arise from a sense of insecurity or inadequacy.

The secure child is one whose needs for affection and belonging have been met. The need for affection is usually satisfied by parental love. It is a rare parent who does not love his child, but some parents hide their love under a cover of indifference. For the sake of the mental health of their children, it is necessary to lift the lid so that children may see and feel the deep well of affection underneath.

Teachers help to satisfy the child's need for affection by a sincere, consistent, and impartial friendliness. When they take a continuous interest in the progress of the individual child, they contribute to the child's feeling of security. The friendly teacher also gives the child a sense of belonging. The child is made to feel that he belongs to a group by being welcomed into a school, by having his birthdays recognized by the group, by having his talents appreciated, by the teacher's interest in his family and his life outside the school, and in other innumerable ways.

The school can make the child feel that he is a success or a failure. On one hand, it may provide opportunities in developmental tasks suited to the child's level of maturity so that every child can feel successful. On the other hand, it may set arbitrary grade standards which are impossible for many children to meet. In the latter, slow-learning children fall by the wayside in frustration. The teacher in the new school tries to heal the wounds of the disturbed child by making him feel worthy in such accomplishments as are suited to his abilities. A teacher who understands children's needs will reject any system of grouping or of evaluation that tends to make one child feel inferior or falsely superior to another. In evaluation she gives more praise than blame. She guides children toward a responsible self-discipline by having them set ever higher goals as they are able.

Meeting individual differences in mental ability. With the almost universal use in our schools of intelligence tests, teachers become aware of the wide range of mental ability in a single classroom— a range which might include the mentally retarded, the dull, the normal, the bright, and the very bright, with occasionally a genius or two. The first reaction of the school to the knowledge of mental differences was to make provision for children at the lower end of the scale. Some slow-learning children were placed in special schools and special classes. Those who remained in the classroom were given more individual attention. It was considerably later that the needs of gifted children were recognized. Special schools, special classes, enrichment programs, and other experiments were started to challenge the gifted children to achieve according to their own potentials.

In an attempt to meet individual differences in mental ability, some schools adopted a plan which placed children in groups (either within the school or within the classroom) according to their intelligence quotients. Over the country as a whole, homogeneous grouping according to mental abilities has been abandoned because the unfavorable emotional effects more than offset any benefits from adjusting subject matter to mental ability. Children in slow-learning groups suffered from feelings of inferiority and lacked the stimulation of contributions that would be present in a normal group, while bright children sometimes developed feelings of undue superiority.

Meeting individual differences in readiness. Some of the first essentials that the teacher considers before teaching subject matter are the following: Are all the children ready for the instructional program of the school? Are they physically, mentally, and emotionally ready? In the physical category, examination of vision and hearing as well as general health are necessary. As to mental ability, children in the general population show such a wide range that some will be slower in pace of learning while others will go faster than the average. Emotional maturity is also a variable. Some children are so insecure that they must be made to consider themselves part of the group and must be given an opportunity to succeed in something they like to do before formal instruction in such a complex subject as reading, for example, is begun.

To the teacher the readiness of children for learning involves two things: maturation or ripening of the organism, and a school readiness program that will aid the child's readiness for learning.

Meeting individual differences in subject-matter achievement. Just as children were found to be different in mental ability, so they also showed a range in achievement in subject matter. Within the first grade, the range may be three or four years and this spread increases with each grade until the span in the sixth grade is eight years in differences of achievement.

Although psychological studies have shown a positive correlation in an individual's ability to succeed in one subject with his ability to succeed in another subject, these correlations vary with different individuals. To illustrate, a child who excels in language arts will tend to excel in arithmetic, but this does not necessarily follow. He may excel in language arts but not in arithmetic or vice versa.

To meet the child's varying subject-matter needs, the schools have tried homogeneous grouping according to subject-matter achievement. Under this plan Jack, who excels in arithmetic achievement but is poor in reading, would be placed in the fast-moving group in arithmetic and a slower-moving group in reading.

It can be readily seen that homogeneous grouping according to subject matter would be more successful in adapting subject matter to individual ability than the plan of homogeneous grouping according to mental ability. Feelings of inferiority or superiority might still be present but in less degree, as superiority in one subject might compensate for inferiority in another. Nevertheless, homogeneous grouping according to subject matter, unless flexibly and sensitively directed by a skilled teacher, has most of the disadvantages of homogeneous grouping according to mental ability.

Meeting individual differences through social promotion. Psychology recognizes the fact that growth and learning are continuous. Many schools follow this psychological principle by what is called *social promotion:* a child moves from grade to grade without repeating a grade. The teacher accepts the child where he is and leads him to further growth. An increasing number of schools realize that children need experiences of success to keep mentally healthy. They therefore are unwilling to stigmatize children as failures by refusing to promote them from one grade to another.

Other schools have adopted a compromise plan called the *Ungraded Primary Plan.* Under this plan grade-designations are abolished. Children progress at their own rates of speed until the end of the third year. At this time children either enter the fourth grade or spend additional time under the primary plan.

The evidence from research studies shows that children do not make as much progress by retardation as they make by promotion to the next grade. They seldom, if ever, do any better by repeating a grade.

In some places where the primary ungraded plan has been tried, evaluation has shown less retardation at the end of three years and better social and emotional adjustment on the part of children than under the traditional fail-or-promote plan. Some schools are extending the ungraded plan to include the intermediate as well as the primary grades.

Meeting individual differences through units of work. One of the best vehicles yet discovered for meeting individual differences is the *unit of work,* which allows all children to contribute to a joint project, each according to his ability. Suitable units of work often originate with the children under the guidance of the teacher. The unit organization permits gifted children to enrich the total learning experience by more extended reading or by other more creative activities, while retarded children can participate in lesser degree but in ways that are valuable to them, and all can feel that they have contributed to the worth of a shared enterprise.

Units of work may also be selected from a course of study. A unit of work may arise spontaneously from a school project, children's hobbies, a happening in nature, or some other source.

Unless properly guided by the teacher, possible drawbacks to units chosen by pupils are that a study may have been chosen that appeals to only a few children rather than the majority, or that time is to be spent on a trivial or relatively unimportant problem from which few values will be derived. To avoid this danger teachers and children, working cooperatively, will consider whether a unit of work meets important goals.

When units are selected from within the flexible framework of a course of study, there is less likelihood that trivial subject matter will be included than when children alone select a unit. But how shall we make children accept such a unit as their own? The key to this problem is in choosing a unit of work that can be adapted to the children's own interests.

After the problem for study has been selected, how does the teacher proceed? If goals have not already emerged, these are now selected insofar as they can be foreseen at the time. These goals may be written upon the chalkboard and later transferred to a wall chart. Should the unit start going off on tangents, reference to the purpose chart can get it back on the track—that is, unless the tangent involves a new pertinent and important value. Then this value may be added to those already proposed.

After setting goals, discussion proceeds as to what data is needed to solve the problem and sub-problems, where to find the data, and who is to be responsible for each task. Charts may be made showing what to do: the books to be read, experiments to be carried out, persons to be interviewed, construction activities to be completed, excursions to be planned, reports to be presented, bibliographies to be kept.

Committees are formed that are usually interest groups with free choice as to membership. The teacher sometimes may suggest a committee assignment when she feels that interpersonal relationships or the learning situation will be improved thereby. For example, she may find that a certain group lacks the leadership needed for the responsibilities undertaken, or she may find that a child who needs practice in research techniques invariably chooses to paint murals. Teachers unaccustomed to working with children in small groups may profitably start committee work with one small group only, instead of with many small groups working simultaneously. Children need to learn the techniques of working together. When the one committee is accustomed to the methods of group action, another group may be formed. The final benefits of small group activities, such as learning to live together and taking pride in group accomplishment, will far outweigh any initial difficulties in organization.

Evaluation is continuous throughout the unit. Sincere praise is given judicially for achievement of goals. Since the group understands that it is working for improvement, the members gather for group evaluation of the progress of the project whenever it is advantageous to reassess goals or to share findings. A final evaluation is made that celebrates the completion of the unit by a program for parents or another class or the school. The program may include reports, reading of creative writings, singing original songs, dramatizations, original moving pictures, and many other events.

The teacher in her own evaluation of the unit of work will note growth in attitudes and values, changes in behavior, individual strengths and weaknesses. She will consider next steps in achieving the goals of education.

A unit provides opportunities for meeting individual differences of children without accompanying feelings of inferiority or superiority that are present in some other attempts to meet individual differences. The unit gives ample scope for creative planning and constructive activities of many types. Children gain more insight by using a problem-solving procedure than by some more conventional methods.

Group Dynamics

Still another trend in today's schools is the use of group dynamics. The term *group dynamics* is relatively new. It refers to the formation and change in the functions and structure of groups. A group exists when two or more people are in interaction with one another. A dynamic group is in a process of continuous change and adjustment so that the members may satisfy their common needs. Sociology, anthropology, and psychology all have contributed experimental material to our knowledge of group dynamics.

One of the earliest experiments by Allport of the effect of the group on the behavior of its members established some important results indicating that more ideas were produced by the group than by individuals when working alone. But "work requiring imagination or more concentrated and original thought is best performed in seclusion."[7]

Another study in the field of group dynamics is that by Deutsch, in which he considers the relative merits of cooperative versus competitive social groups.[8] In the cooperative social situation, the members tend to help each other's progress, to show more organizational flexibility, to have stronger motivation toward the goal, better interpersonal relations, and more group productivity.

The interrelationship among the members of a group creates a distinctive climate. When this relationship is democratic, then the democratic climate prevails.[9] Studies of ten-year-old boys and three different types of club leaders—the autocratic, the laissez-faire, and the democratic—showed the effect of climate upon work and behavior of boys. On the surface, autocratic direction yielded quick and orderly results, but the atmosphere of the group soon changed under the authoritarian rules of the leader. Faces of the boys that had been aglow with interest became apathetic. The rigid discipline that prevailed in the clubroom under the authoritarian rule disintegrated when the dictator was absent from the room, and the boys showed hostility and aggression toward one another.

The laissez-faire leader allowed the group complete freedom in choice of procedure and choice of workmates. The boys were slow in beginning their work and soon disruptive behavior prevented the completion of the project.

The democratic leader encouraged the planning of policies and procedures. The interest of the group in their work was intense and lasting. The group accomplished more and maintained a friendly

---

[7] F. H. Allport, "The Influence of the Group Upon Association and Thought," *Journal of Experimental Psychology,* No. 3 (1920), pp. 159–82.

[8] Morton Deutsch, "The Effects of Cooperation and Competition Upon Group Process," *Human Relations,* No. 2 (1949), pp. 129–52, 199–231.

[9] K. Lewin, Ronald Lippitt, and R. K. White, "Patterns of Behavior in Experimentally Created Social Climates," *Journal of Social Psychology,* No. 10 (1939), pp. 271–99.

behavior toward one another throughout. When the leader left the room the work continued as before.

Durrell reports a recent experiment in grouping by teams of two or three pupils who were paired in ability, and who were permitted to progress in arithmetic and spelling as rapidly as they could demonstrate mastery. Study guides were provided for teams in reading, history, and geography. Durrell reported a difference in the adaptability of school subjects to this type of organization. The skill subjects adapted readily while the content subjects were less satisfactorily adjusted. The program resulted in significant improvement in achievement in grades five and six; no change was found in grade four.[10]

Valuable as is the group to the child, group organization must be balanced with individual activities. Studies have shown that the child can concentrate better apart from the group and show more originality and imagination. A tendency of the group to demand conformity at the expense of individuality of expression and action needs to be carefully watched in group processes. Too extreme a group integration can have the undesirable effect of undermining the individual's initiative. Excessive evaluating, for example, may cause the individual to prefer silence to continual criticism of his ideas.

Children of different social classes have different values. Behavior that meets with approval in one social class may meet with disapproval in another. Observation has shown that children of one social class will profit from social contact with children of other social classes only as they meet with acceptance by their own peers.

Membership within small groups is a benefit to both the shy and the aggressive child. A shy child may be willing to express himself more freely in a small group, whereas he may have retreated more and more into himself while in the large group. Within the small group his freer expression is invaluable in preventing mental disturbances.

The overly aggressive child may also profit from inclusion in a small group. Here he may get the attention he needs and a realization of what talents he possesses. He will profit by the democratic procedures and gradually moderate his tendency toward dominance and the use of attention-getting devices.

---

[10] Donald Durrell, "Adapting Instruction to the Learning Needs of Children," *Journal of Education*, Vol. 42, No. 2 (December, 1959), p. 5.

Where a large group is at work on a school project, it is often broken up into small committees. Each committee is motivated to make a good showing in reporting back to the committee of the whole. This stimulation of a group enterprise spurs the entire committee until its job is finished. Praise by their own peers for a job well done counts more with youngsters than praise from adults.

Socially integrative behavior is furthered when the individual grows in understanding of group welfare and at the same time maintains his own uniqueness. This is best accomplished through group experiences in which the individual child is accepted *as he is*. Through group processes children are drawn together by similar interests, by peer friendships, by the setting of common goals, by committee activity in which several children share the work for group purposes, and by appreciative evaluation of the accomplishments of the group.

Sociometric and Projective Techniques

To help teachers understand children's friendship patterns and other problems of adjustment, both sociometric and projective techniques are used. Sociometric techniques are a comparatively recent innovation in the schools. Sociometry includes sociometric testing and questionnaires. Projective techniques include sociodrama, play therapy, and free creative expression.

Sociometry measures each pupil's interpersonal likes and dislikes. Typical questions asked of each pupil are: "With whom do you like to work?" or "With whom do you like to play?" Choices may be limited to a specific number of persons or the number of choices may be unlimited.

Again, a child may be asked to list his best friends. Such a questionnaire helps the teacher discover the general acceptance or rejection of members of the class. This data may be used by the teacher for sociometric grouping in which the teacher may try to bring feelings of belonging to those with no friends, to increase mutuality of friendships, to expand closely knit groups, and to improve work efficiency and enjoyment of members of the group.

Sociometric data may be arranged either in a sociometric chart, sometimes called a sociogram, or in a matrix chart. The sociometric chart may use squares to represent boys, circles for girls, arrows (for single choices), and double arrows (for mutual choices). Isolates (those who are unchosen) are placed on the periphery of the chart, stars (those who are outstanding in number of choices) are placed in the center, and others fall between. These charts, because of their pictorial nature, are vivid and appealing but they take considerable time in the making.

A matrix chart lists names of the class members vertically while choice data for each class member are presented horizontally. Such a chart can be quickly made and includes all pertinent information. The worthy goal of sociometry is improvement of interpersonal relations. The questions, however, may focus pupils' attention upon unfriendly, rather than friendly, relationships within the class.

Projective techniques are used to reveal children's unfulfilled needs. They may not only disclose the child's need but also free him from tension and thus help to put him on the road to normality. In all the projective procedures almost complete freedom of action is allowed.

In sociodrama a child may be assigned a role such as that of a father, son, king, or hero. He is allowed freedom in his interpretation of the role without fear of criticism or ridicule. When the teacher considers it desirable, the child may play a role that is the reverse of a previous one. This double acting may give him two points of view as, for example, in a father-and-son relationship.

In play therapy a child plays freely with a number of toys, talking to them and handling them as he pleases. In the course of time he may reveal to the teacher-therapist the unfulfilled need which has been causing his emotional disturbance. In freely playing out his feelings he may be relieved of tensions and negative emotions. A similar release from tensions may result from creative expression in art, music, writing, dancing, or other arts. Here, too, the child may reveal unfulfilled needs. He must feel the same kind of security in expression as is allowed in play therapy or sociodrama.

The teacher, as therapist, may not always have time to analyze causes of an individual's mental and emotional disturbances before taking action. At times a child's behavior may endanger the safety and well being of the thirty or more children who are also in the room. Immediate action such as a child's isolation from the others may be necessary. Later the teacher may seek the reasons for the behavior. The causes of behavior are so complex that they are not always easy to determine, and in severe cases the teacher will refer the disturbed child to persons especially trained in emotional disorders for more extended therapy. During successful therapy there is a tendency toward acceptance of the self on the part of the child.

According to Carl Rogers, acceptance of the self means that the client tends:

> To perceive himself as a person of worth, worthy of respect rather than condemnation.
>
> To perceive his standards as being based upon his own experience rather than upon the attitudes or desires of others.
>
> To perceive his own feelings, motives, social and personal experiences, without distortion of the basic sensory data.[11]

Through sociometric testing and questionnaires the teacher learns better to understand her children; she obtains a better perception of a child's social status and aspirations as well as his general acceptance or rejection by his peers. She uses this knowledge for sociometric grouping, which has several advantages over other kinds of grouping. She tries to win acceptance for the child previously rejected by his peers. She uses ego-building methods so that each child may have feelings of "counting for something." Through projective techniques she provides acceptable release of the emotions. She makes the classroom a wholesome and happy place in which to live.

Some schools, in attempting student government, organize children's courts to try students who do not live by the rule. These courts mete out punishments for various offenses. Since aggressive behavior is often the result of consciousness of inferiority, punishment for aggression may aggravate the original cause rather than prevent it. Moreover, children do not have the maturity to analyze or prescribe for behavior difficulties. Better practices do not in general recommend punishments for misbehaviors.

Evaluation of the democratic procedures are necessary from time to time. Fairness would dictate that certain children cannot monopolize the agreeable jobs, but that all must share equally in all kinds of work. Therefore some classrooms may decide upon rotation of jobs from week to week or some other scheme of distribution of responsibility.

When children help to plan units of work and are permitted some reasonable choice of task assignments and committee work, a cooperative spirit develops that needs no motivation of extrinsic rewards. A task is completed on time so that one's committee will

---

[11] Carl Rogers, "The Significance of the Self-Regarding Attitudes and Perceptions," in Reymert, M. L., *Feelings and Emotions* (New York: McGraw-Hill Book Company, Inc., 1950), pp. 376–77. With permission.

not be disappointed. A loyalty to the group devolves. Good workmanship is prized, and excellence of many kinds is recognized. In such democratic classrooms all children, no matter what their mental ability may be, can feel that they have contributed to the general good. Children trained to make rules and to obey them will realize the necessity of laws for the public welfare, and more heedful obedience to those laws. This is training in patriotism of the highest order. As future citizens, individuals from democratic schools will not fall easy prey to demagogues or misleading propaganda. They will make more thoughtful decisions because they have practiced democracy in a wide variety of experiences. Through wise guidance in group processes the individual learns to work with the group rather than against it.

The Scientific Method

Any subject area may use the scientific method of thinking. Science has emphasized this procedure to such an extent that the method has received its name from that area. The scientific method is one which considers all sides of a question before coming to conclusions; it bases judgment upon the evidence and not upon prejudice; it requires proof for all its findings.

The scientific method is frequently analyzed into the following steps:

1. Finding the problem and defining it.
2. Forming hypothesis as to outcomes.
3. Gathering data related to the problem, experimenting, demonstrating, and retesting.
4. Generalizing or coming to conclusions based on the data.
5. Appreciation of the generalizations.
6. Applications.

The procedure in the scientific method closely resembles that practiced in units of work—the finding of a problem, the gathering of data, and the final generalizing and evaluating.

The scientific method regards conclusions as tentative because absolute conclusions might be upset by future discoveries. The present respected status of science and the scientific method is partly owing to the fact that science does not make any unverifiable claims. When children are trained in the scientific method of thought, they have a way of thinking that can be applied to the solution of any problem. They will want to hear all sides of a question before forming judgments. They will learn that the consequences of an erroneous decision may be disastrous.

Discipline

Discipline is the control of behavior in accordance with the acceptable standards of society. A disciplined person considers the consequence of his action before he acts. In the autocratic climate, discipline may be very strict; in the laissez-faire classroom, very permissive; in the democratic classroom, self-governed. The authoritarian teacher expects to have absolute control and submissive obedience. Under laissez-faire, extreme permissiveness and great freedom of action prevail. Research studies show that both authoritarian and laissez-faire discipline produce disastrous results. In Frenkel-Brunswik's study, children whose scores indicated extreme prejudice were outwardly submissive to authority but inwardly resentful and rebellious.[12]

Today, we teach children to obey, but we want this obedience to be a thinking obedience, not merely a reliance upon authority. Children are led gradually to discipline themselves. The self-disciplined child is likely to behave in satisfactory ways whether the teacher is present or absent from the room.

Children are taught that there is a time for quiet and a time for activity, a time to converse and a time to listen, a time to work and a time to relax. Such a classroom presents a better mental-hygiene picture than one in which children are kept at a high speed of endeavor throughout the school day.

Teachers realize that many disturbed children come into the classroom. These children display hostility, indifference, or withdrawal. Good teachers accept both intellectually and emotionally all kinds of children. They do not show resentment toward or condemnation of children who misbehave.

In the democratic classroom a reasonable amount of freedom is allowed. Children are led to develop a sense of responsibility along with liberty. Here discipline involves the formulation of rules of conduct by the children and evaluation of behavior in accordance with their own goals of conduct. Children are taught to place emphasis on the positive rather than the negative, on *do* rather than

---

[12] Else Frenkel-Brunswik, "Further Contributions by a Contributor," *Studies in the Scope and Method of The Authoritarian Personality,* eds. Richard Christie and Marie Johoda (Glencoe, Ill.: The Free Press, 1954), pp. 264–65.

don't. Sometimes the classroom's code of behavior is hung in sight for all to see, and at the close of each day behavior of the class is considered in the light of the code of behavior. Group conduct becomes of supreme importance; the misbehavior of even one individual in the group that is reporting makes a poor group report. It is not necessary to name the miscreant; he feels the displeasure of his peers and tries to improve the group record on the next report. Cooperative activities are an aid to discipline. A shared project usually means interested interaction among pupils.

Good management of the classroom activities avoids confusion and contributes to orderliness. Materials of instruction are readily available. A clear understanding of what to do and where to do it are other aids. Alternate periods of activity with opportunities for relaxation are better than too close concentration of study. When class work is finished ahead of time, choice of free activities keeps those children who finish early occupied and out of mischief.

Children learn right ways of conduct by acting in the right manner. The activity school provides opportunities for right action to a greater degree than does the listening school. Many schools build up traditions of high values. Repeated performances of right action lead to good habits. The teacher who is a skilled disciplinarian integrates character education into every learning situation.

Some children continually disrupt the classroom with negative behavior of one kind or another. The teacher's guidance of individual behavior is made in private. First she establishes a friendly relationship with the child. She makes certain that he understands why his conduct is unacceptable behavior. Together, teacher and pupil plan remedial action. An occasion is provided in the near future for making a correct response. A report on the performance of the accepted behavior is made to the teacher. The child notes other occasions when he has made the correct response. Eventually the new and accepted behavior replaces the old unaccepted conduct.

An aspect of discipline that children have to learn is that personal contacts involve a control of behavior toward others so as to promote satisfaction to all parties. Each person needs to have as much freedom of thought and action as is not in interference with the genuine welfare of the others. Promotion of this kind of responsible liberty is an outstanding feature of modern schools. Children are given the freedom of speech and action that become the good habits of an adult democratic society. Finally, the child must learn a discipline in harmony with the culture in which he lives. In any culture, many sociological, economic, and political forces operate, some positive, others negative. An individual within the culture must learn to control his behavior so as to secure a reasonable degree of conformity and at the same time a desirable drive toward the improvement of forces inimicable to the welfare of society. Toward achievement of this type of discipline, children make beginnings both through their study of social problems and through service projects, not only in the school but in the community.

There was a time when discipline decreed that children should be seen and not heard. Then, a teacher who could keep a classroom so quiet that you could hear a pin drop was considered the best disciplinarian. As William Heard Kilpatrick has pointed out, a worse condition for character building would be hard to find. When children are learning to live together in groups, absolute quiet is virtually impossible.

Teachers, administrators, and the public must realize that some adult comfort in matters of discipline must be sacrificed to the greater good of child welfare. Many schools in attempting newer types of procedures would like the advantages that follow from group processes but would still retain the quietness of the old regime. True, a too abrupt change from authoritarian controls to more democratic ways may result in an outburst of overt misbehavior when liberty is granted. Therefore, a more gradual release of adult controls as children are able to assume responsibility is to be recommended. A friendly but firm discipline is usually best as children are moving in the direction of improved behaviors. Children do not come to school as mature individuals with fully developed controls of behavior; they have to learn self discipline just as they have to learn how to read.

To learn right behavior one must act in right ways—not once, but again and again until the right behavior becomes habit. One of the great rewards of the teaching profession is to observe the child's forward strides toward maturity of behavior.

Praise has been found to be more effective than blame. The use of punishment is questionable in the control of behavior because of the fact that it may have exactly the opposite effect to the one desired. Several negative disciplinary procedures that are now seldom, if ever, used in newer type schools are imposition of school assignments for infringement of rules, keeping a child after school as a punishment, forced apologies, and corporal punishment. Temporary exclusion of a member from the class, although not desirable as a general practice, may be necessary at times for the safety and welfare of the rest of the children. Very disturbed children should be referred to a psychological clinic for diagnosis and treatment.

Newer Materials and Modes of Instruction

With the advent of bus transportation for school children, instruction which had formerly been contained within the four walls of the classroom expanded to include the community. At almost the same time the invention of radio and television beamed the outside world into the classroom.

Audio-visual materials. The new materials of instruction that appeal to the ear and the eye are called audio-visual aids. They include radio, television, films, film strips, moving pictures, recordings, and other community resources. The term audio-visual materials also embraces kinesthetic objects that can be touched and handled by the children.

Since, from earliest infancy, most of our knowledge comes to us primarily through the use of the five senses of sight, hearing, touch, smell, and taste, it follows that the introduction into the schools of materials making use of one or more of these senses confers upon learning a reality not so easily come by through books alone.

Research has shown an increase in the number of facts learned from audio-visual materials over the number of facts learned by traditional methods. Also, facts learned from audio-visual materials were retained for a significantly longer period of time. Some evidence exists in support of more accurate knowledge of concepts learned through audio-visual materials rather than through textbooks. Also, training in certain skills through audio-visual aids has been highly successful as was demonstrated by the armed forces in World War II.

Audio-visual materials such as films often have emotional connotations that help boys and girls understand the important values of the culture. However, changes in attitudes seldom result from the showing of one film, but the use of several films designed for the purpose of inculcating values have resulted in pronounced changes in behavior. Audio-visual aids have some very special advantages. By the use of time-lapse photography, time can be compressed so that in a few moments, children can see the sprouting, blooming, and fading of a flower. Also, time relationships can be shown to better advantage through a sequence of events in an historical film than in any other medium.

Audio aids, or those which use hearing as the principal avenue of perception, are radio, phonograph records, tape recordings, sound effects, and musical instruments.

Visual aids, or those which appeal predominantly to the eye, are maps, globes, diagrams, films, film strips, and television. Programs on television which are beamed into classrooms are gaining in popularity. The teacher who presents the lesson through television is called a television teacher. The television teacher is an expert in her subject and through television can teach in many classrooms at the same time. She faces the camera and on the screen seems to be looking directly at the boys and girls in the classrooms.

Examples of kinesthetic experiences are tracing letters or words in a sandbox, using a felt board and felt objects, working with clay or finger paints, and constructing with other craft materials.

When audio-visual materials are used in connection with other activities of the classroom, their effectiveness is increased. Integration of learning materials has long been recognized as one of the techniques of better schools. Audio-visual aids may be used to motivate a project, to provide data, and to summarize learnings.

Research has found that the effectiveness of audio-visual aids is increased when children help set the purposes and thus identify themselves with the learning situation. Preparation may include stating and defining a problem, suggesting possible consequences, and forming hypotheses. Also beneficial is a follow-up of an audio-visual presentation. After the use of audio-visual aids, important factors may be discussed; generalizations may be formulated; applications may be drawn; and expression in one or more of the creative arts may help to bring unity and completeness to the entire experience. Evaluation of materials by children will help them to discard the shoddy and harmful and to appreciate the significant and helpful.

Both listening and looking skills must be taught in order to obtain the maximum benefit from audio-visual materials. Children are likely to hear what they have been trained to hear. In recent school practice, listening has been stressed not as a passive but purposeful act. Appreciation of beauty in music can be increased when the child knows how to listen to good music. Enjoyment of good speech is multiplied with knowledge of speech skills. A highly desirable result of evaluation of listening experiences will be an improvement in the selection of radio and television programs by children.

Just as there are special skills in listening, so there are special skills in looking that need to be learned. Pupils learn to look at pictures so that relationships as well as isolated details may be perceived. They learn how to interpret symbols on a map, how to understand various types of graphs, how to arrange an attractive bulletin board, how to publish a classroom newspaper, how to demonstrate an experiment, and how to collect and preserve specimens for a science museum.

Experiments in educational television have yielded some startling results according to Paul R. Wendt. He reports as follows:

> Since TV teaching is done almost always by the best teachers available, it is not surprising that it can overcome the impersonality and mechanical nature of children's learning from a TV set. Most of the experiments have shown TV teaching to be an effective help to the classroom teacher.
>
> More radical are the recent and current experiments of teaching by television alone without any instruction from a classroom teacher. Subjects from second-grade spelling to college psychology have been taught solely by a teacher on a TV screen. In every controlled experiment the students learned as much as from classroom instruction. This shocking result may be turned by wise teachers to their own advantage if they allow the machine to expound facts and demonstrate skills. Thus they could free themselves to devote their trained and experienced abilities into guiding students and individualizing instruction.[18]

During the 1950's, the most startling innovation in newer materials of instruction was the introduction of machines into the schools. These machines offered instruction that has been termed *programmed* learning. Programmed learning gave instruction in planned sequence and in simple graduated steps. Instead of testing the pupil at the completion of a lesson, the machine tests him at every step. The pupil makes a response by filling in a blank or by pushing a button. The machine "rewards" the pupil with an immediate acknowledgment of the correct answer.

---

[18] Paul R. Wendt, "What Research Says to the Teacher," *Audio-Visual Instruction*, No. 14 (Washington, D.C.: National Education Association, December, 1957), p. 28. Prepared by the American Educational Research Association in cooperation with the Department of Classroom Teachers.

Machines help in providing individual instruction to meet varying rates of speed ability. A bright learner can move at a rapid pace while the slow learner may take as long as he needs. One claim made for the machine is that it makes for speedy accurate learning. Another advantage claimed for the machine is that a relatively complex subject can be learned by pupils at an earlier age than would otherwise be possible.

A disadvantage is the relatively high cost of many machines. Therefore substitutes for the machine are being provided in the form of workbooks with shields and answer slides that use the same or similar methods of programming.

Field trips. All the rich resources of the community become available to children when they can go together on excursions or field trips away from the schoolroom and into the immediate neighborhood, nearby communities, or distant parts of the country. Formerly, resource visitors from the community occasionally visited the school to share some of their experiences with boys and girls, but field trips made possible a much more frequent contact with resource persons. Collections of objects in museums, and art in nearby galleries enriched the learning experiences of children. Historical spots could be visited. Industries, business establishments, and even some homes opened their doors to help expand learning. Children could at times attend a rare musical performance or an outstanding theatrical production. The possibilities for experiences were as wide as life itself.

A school trip is undertaken for specific purposes. Like personal travel it can in itself be both enjoyable and informative as new places, things, and persons present themselves. The school trip is tied in with the school curriculum. Sometimes the purpose is to motivate a new project. Again, it is to get information at first hand regarding a unit of work. The field trip seeks to provide emotional meaning to otherwise purely verbal knowledge and to lead the child into an understanding of distinctive values of the community.

Disadvantages of field trips lie principally in the time consumed by the excursion. The advantages, therefore, have to outweigh the disadvantages. When field trips can provide information not to be obtained in books, then they can add a reality and interest that make the school curriculum a living thing. When the acquisition of important community values leads to improved behavior, then economy of time cannot be considered the most important factor.

Various types of field trips make contributions to the learning situation in the classroom. At times children visit a historical site such as the home of a famous man, or they study a geographical phenomena such as the geological evidence left by a glacial age. Again, they visit a museum to ascertain how people lived in the past. At another time a field trip may have as its goal getting acquainted with children of another school, people of another race, an aged person who cannot come to the school but who has a vivid memory of folklore and community history. Almost any field trip holds the probability of contact with people and pleasant experiences in gracious, courteous, and kind behavior.

Usually, preparation for a field trip involves an understanding of why the trip is being undertaken and what to look for on the trip. When the purpose is to arouse interest in a new unit, little previous discussion will be needed. But in preparation, children may write letters asking permission for the visit, both from their parents and from resource persons who are to be visited. The school typically asks written permission from parents for a child's participation on an excursion. After the trip, children write thank-you letters for courtesies shown them. Rules of safe behavior are agreed upon by children and teacher. When the children return to school, aspects of the trip that are related directly to the purpose of the excursion will be discussed and the trip evaluated. Children and parents as well as teachers need to understand why field trips are worthwhile. Free expression after a field trip will often result in creative writing of prose and verse, individual paintings and group murals, musical composition and other forms of expression. The motivating force of the excursion may remain for days and even weeks and provoke much reading and study.

Methods of Appraisal

Measurement and evaluation go hand-in-hand as methods of appraisal but are not synonymous. Measurement connotes something quantitative whereas evaluation emphasizes quality. The measurement movement in the elementary schools seems to be on the decline, and evaluation in the ascendancy.

Measurement. The measurement movement began near the close of the nineteenth century when J. M. Rice startled the educational world with his experiments in spelling in which he demonstrated that pupils who devoted fifteen minutes per day to spelling could do just as well on spelling tests as those who devoted forty minutes per day to the subject. In the first half of the twentieth century the measurement movement spread rapidly. An analysis of tests may be found in Buros' *Fifth Mental Measurements Year-book*.[14]

Standardized tests that came to be widely used in schools to measure progress in subject-matter areas are called achievement tests. A battery of tests to include many areas became popular. Achievement tests show present norms of achievement for each grade and for each subject tested. These tests are used for comparison of one school system with another, of one experimental group with a control group, of classes using different methods of instruction, and for analyzing an individual child's progress and future needs.

With all their advantages, achievement tests have several shortcomings: the questions may not conform to the curriculum requirements in the school being tested; the tests have centered attention upon academic achievement to the detriment of other important goals of instruction; they have made progress in learning quantitative rather than qualitative. For these reasons evaluation, which embraces quality as well as quantity, is replacing the former emphasis upon measurement.

Evaluation. Evaluation had to triumph over measurement because of the multiple educational goals, many of which are incapable of exact measurement. Whereas academic achievement is fairly easy to measure, other goals such as acquisition of cultural values and improvement of behavior do not yield so readily to quantitative scoring.

Both the teacher and pupils take a cooperative part in evaluation. When pupils formulate the goals for a project, the teacher guides them in evaluation of those goals. She sees that pupils consider the progress of a project and helps them to set new goals in addition to those already formulated. The children's final report on a project always includes evaluation of the project in which they judge whether goals have been accomplished and what new goals lie ahead. Thus evaluation in modern schools becomes both foresight and hindsight.

---

[14] Oscar K. Buros, *The Fifth Mental Measurements Yearbook* (Highland Park, New Jersey: Gryphon Press, 1959).

Included in evaluation are information gained, changes in attitudes, opinions, and habits of working, as well as other improvements in behavior. Generalizations are made on the basis of the data learned, and applications are made in a wide variety of situations. This continuous evaluation is training that leads to more mature thinking and reasoning. Therefore moral values are taken out of the realm of abstraction and become a vital part of the lives of boys and girls. The child comes to feel his own responsibility to himself and to society.

Tests to evaluate aspects of learning other than intelligence and achievement of subject matter are still in the experimental stage. But even in their present experimental stage, they are often useful in appraising the less tangible aspects of education. Such tests include interest tests, personal and social adjustment tests, and sociometric tests. Aptitude tests measure talent for a given activity such as music, art, or mechanical ability. Personal and social adjustment tests attempt to discover personal problems and personal traits. Friendship patterns are revealed by sociometric tests.

Since evaluation involves quality of living as well as academic achievement, the old system of reporting to parents in terms of academic grades alone is indefensible. Experiments with newer forms of reporting have included letters and conferences with parents in the belief that elaboration of appraisal could explain the new goals better than the symbols formerly used on report cards. Through the newer types of reporting, better cooperative action between home and school is often attained.

A present promising trend in evaluation is to express attitudes in terms of readily identifiable behaviors. For example, a cooperative attitude may result in the following behaviors: "responds readily to requests," "volunteers his assistance," "initiates projects to bring about improvement." With this focus on specific improvements teachers, parents, and pupils can more readily determine the progress in better attitudes.

A leader in the evaluation movement is J. Wayne Wrightstone, who in the thirties developed procedures for assessing intangibles. In 1936 the Eight-Year Study of Progressive Education used evaluative techniques in its experiment to assess the outcomes of traditional and new-type schools.

Another promising trend in evaluation is self-evaluation by the learner. When children sense their own progress, they are more likely to succeed. By evaluating themselves, under wise guidance, children realize their own relationship to their group.

Education is excellent when it helps a child grow from weakness to strength and from immaturity to maturity. An effective education makes each child appreciate his own worth as an individual and his own responsibility in the democratic culture. With such education the modern teacher can say with earnest belief what another democratic teacher has so poetically phrased:

> I will make the most splendid race the sun ever shone upon,
> I will make divine magnetic lands.
> I will plant companionship thick as trees.[15]

A child's progress must be considered in relationship to the obstacles he has overcome. Competitive grading that makes one child feel inferior during all his formative years because he cannot move as fast as children with higher intelligence quotients has no place in a democracy. Every child needs to have awareness of success, and learning experiences should be provided in which *he can succeed*. Any system of evaluation that discriminates against any group of children for any reason whether psychological (as in the case of the slow learner), physical, or social, is indefensibly undemocratic.

---

[15] Walt Whitman, *Leaves of Grass* (Boston: Thayer and Eldridge, 1860–61), p. 351.

CHAPTER III

Teaching Practices
in Subject-Matter Areas

Education in a culture that is changing as rapidly as is the technology of today needs to be alert to necessary changes in its schools lest there be too great a lag between the dynamic culture and the education of boys and girls. Schools have to select what is considered as most worthy. The selected knowledge and skills must be arranged in a sequence from one grade to another.

In order to meet the individual differences among children, mass instruction is inadequate. Therefore, schools provide a flexible framework or guide from which the teacher has opportunity to select those experiences that best meet the needs and abilities of individual children. Without a guide there might be wasteful repetition of activities or elimination of some experiences that are considered fundamental and worthy.

Much thought and planning must go into the designed framework for a good school in order to meet the objectives, the developmental needs of children, and the needs of society. A tremendous challenge still lies ahead as to how to proceed in the actual teaching-learning situation for the most effective instruction. Psychology, sociology, and philosophy all serve to guide teachers with their findings as to the best ways by which children learn.

An important research finding that has changed methods of teaching and learning is that problems of life cannot be solved by one subject-matter area alone. Therefore, a number of experimental methods have been used that relate one subject to another or unite all subjects in the learning experience. These experimental methods are correlation, broad fields, integration, and the experience method.

Correlation of subject matter was one of the first attempts to move away from separate subjects; it attempted to show relationships between at least two subject areas. For example, a class studying the early American Indians in history might read *The Last of the Mohicans* for English.

Still later, subjects that were closely related were taught as broad fields. To illustrate, reading and writing, speaking and listening were taught as the language arts. Also, history, geography, and civics became the social studies.

The term *broad fields* has been used interchangeably in educational literature with the term *fusion*. Fusion is defined as the uniting of several areas of subject matter under one title.

Still another method called *integration* seeks to eliminate separate subjects and unify learning. The approach is one of problem-solving, and data is sought wherever it may be found, irrespective of subject-matter distinctions.

An approach closely allied to integration is the experience method in which the emphasis is upon psychological growth rather than upon the unity of subject matter. The experience method uses activities as closely related to real life experiences as possible. Instead of verbal learning only, the child learns to do by doing.

Teachers may at one time use one of these types of procedures and at another time a different type. When children are learning communication skills, a broad-field approach works well. In a study of the community, the experience method is very effective.

A common type of organization is that of broad fields. Language arts will be the first broad field to be discussed.

Language Arts in the Elementary School

The language arts are communication through speaking and listening, reading and writing. A close relationship exists between speaking and listening for the reason that someone speaks because another is listening, and someone listens because another is speaking. A similar close tie binds reading and writing. Someone reads to ascertain what another has written, and someone writes that another may read. Thus, reading and writing, speaking and listening are the media of communication. What is communicated through these media are the inner depths of experiences. Ideas and feelings are the backbone of the language arts program; they arise from the experiences of boys and girls both within and without the school. The richer those experiences, the fuller will be the pupils' expression and the more sensitive their listening.

In integrated programs where children plan, discuss, choose, report, and evaluate, the language arts have a wide variety of outlets. Children are encouraged to seek content for their expression from the area of their interests.

Not only does the child learn that he must have something to say but also a purpose in saying it. Since others are to listen to find out his attitudes, he must consider his audience and the effect the communication is likely to have. Listeners, in turn, will learn to appreciate what is said and how it is said.

Research supports the teaching of language arts as communication rather than as separate subjects. Summaries of this type of research are reported by the National Conference of Research in English[1] and the Commission on the English Curriculum of the National Council of Teachers of English.[2]

Speaking. Speech activities take place in an audience situation where others listen to ascertain the speaker's ideas and convictions. Such activities provide better motivation for speaking and listening than the old method of the recitation of textbook material, which all pupils had read. Speech activities in the early primary grades include telling an event that happened outside school hours, storytelling, dramatizing, conversing, planning, and oral reading.

In the upper primary and intermediate grades additional experiences are discussing, reporting, interviewing, sharing book reports, making tape recordings, telephoning, giving directions, introducing people, improving language usage, extending vocabulary, broadcasting, and evaluating.

Desirable qualities in speech are earnestness, imagination, spontaneity, and a reasonable conformity to the standards of good usage. Teachers endeavor to encourage all of these traits but realize that too strict an emphasis upon standards of conformity may threaten all the other desirable qualities. They provide a balance among these objectives by appreciating the child's present speech development and then leading him on to next steps as he is ready. Criticisms are made in private and not while the child is before the group. The manner of speech is an expression of the self and too severe a criticism may make the child feel unsure of himself.

The speech activities of the school closely approximate the speech activities of the community. Children learn to make phone calls. They practice introducing one child to another, one child to an

---

[1] National Conference on Research in English, *Interrelations Among the Language Arts* (National Council of Teachers of English, 1954).

[2] National Council of Teachers of English, Commission on the English Curriculum, *Language Arts for Today's Children* (New York: Appleton-Century-Crofts, Inc., 1954).

adult, and one adult to another. Other experiences include the giving of cheerful greetings, acknowledging gifts, contributing to a conversation. These social amenities are sometimes learned through dramatization. When a child assumes different roles in the dramatization, he may come to an understanding of different viewpoints, for example, those of a hero, a ruler, and a slave.

Preparing and giving radio or television broadcasts on current events or other subjects provide for a larger audience than that of the classroom. Some schools rotate opportunities for expression through daily broadcasts among the rooms of the school.

Purposeful speech activities in units of work include selecting the unit, stating purposes, discussing activities, preparing oral reports, and evaluating the experiences of the unit. Through these purposeful activities children look for material related to their school work.

As to grammar and good usage, research has shown that time spent on grammar could more effectively be spent on practice of good usage.[3] What kinds of usage shall be taught—the literary forms or the colloquial? The opinion of speech authorities is that the speech goal in the school should be the informal usage of the educated persons of the community. Young children have a vivid speech of their own which is quite adequate for their own purposes and often quite delightfully imaginative. There is no one correct speech; rather, good usage depends upon the occasion of its use.

Listening. Listening takes place during the entire day, but in school it receives special emphasis as part of the language-arts program. Listening involves discovering the opinions and emotions of a speaker. Listening with definite objectives in mind and with attention is not a passive quality. The goals may be to gather data that will help solve a problem or to appreciate a piece of literature. Listening for appreciation may be rapt or relaxed. Certain it is that children listen with more concentration when they either have set the purposes themselves or have accepted the school's purposes as their own.

Listening involves certain courtesies—paying attention, not interrupting in the midst of a sentence or train of thought, and responding when the need arises.

---

3 Walter Logan, "Studies of Language Which Assist the Teacher," *English Journal,* No. 36 (1947), pp. 518–23. See also Fred G. Walcott, "The Limitations of Grammar," University of Michigan School of Education Bulletin 19 (1948), p. 49.

Many children today listen to mass media as much as several hours per day. In order that time be wisely spent, children are taught how to select that which is worthwhile from that which is harmful. They are advised in advance of coming good programs. When educational television is beamed into the classrooms, children listen for material related to their school work.

Reading. Since reading involves discerning the writer's ideas, it becomes a more complex learning experience than mere saying of words.

Reading is taught not only as a skill but also as a means toward the growth of children in confidence, in ability to think, and in the practice of problem solving. Effective teaching of reading is directly aimed at accomplishing a wide variety of purposes needed by the alert individual and the intelligent citizen.

Children come to school eager to learn to read. Some are ready for the teaching of reading upon school entry. Others are not sufficiently mature physically, mentally, emotionally, and socially. For these children, a reading-readiness program precedes the actual teaching of reading. Because factors other than the mental aspect affect this readiness, no mental age for successful learning of reading can be specified.

The teacher provides experiences that will help children get ready to read. Related language activities such as correct usage, clear pronunciation of words, development of sensory acuity, listening with attention, following directions, seeing likenesses and differences in words, and visual discrimination of word elements are readiness activities. Physical defects are corrected whenever possible. The teacher uses both her own observation and a standardized reading-readiness test to determine the child's readiness for reading.

More time is devoted to teaching reading in first grade than any other. The length of the reading period gradually decreases with each grade thereafter. The primary grades usually devote two periods per day to reading, one in the morning and another after lunch.

Methods of reading instruction. In organizing the class for teaching, the teacher uses both individual and group instruction in order to meet the needs, interests, and abilities of the group. Mass instruction will not meet these varying needs; slow children will fall behind and the very bright will be left unchallenged.

Group instruction is used for stimulation of interest, group planning, discussion, evaluation. Small groups are used for economy of instruction when the members of the group have the same or similar needs or interests. Grouping alone is not a method that insures perfect results nor does it produce homogeneity, for differences will exist in even one reading trait as well as among several traits. Research reveals that a teacher's knowledge of children and of methods of teaching them are the major factors for success in teaching children to read.

In any kind of grouping, care must be exercised so that some children do not feel inferior or others unduly superior. The emotional disadvantages in many instances far outweigh any advantages that come from adjusting subject matter to abilities. Grouping still remains a controversial issue. A number of schools and a few school systems are using non-graded reading levels to replace grade reading levels. Children do not repeat grades but move on continuously from year to year according to their growth in reading. This plan has been used chiefly in the primary grades, which are organized into an ungraded primary unit. In the United States nine school systems were classified as having this type of structure in the lower grades in all of their elementary schools.[4]

Several plans for individualized reading instruction that employ a self-selection method of reading materials are presently being tried in the schools. Although the plans differ as to organization and methods, they all agree on the children's free choice of reading materials. Three experimental-controlled studies reported by Dietrich showed that the free-choice groups, as compared to the control groups, made the same, or better, scores in reading achievement. One of these studies reported that the free-choice group showed "new interest in reading and in books."[5]

Children need to be taught certain clues to help them solve the intricate puzzle of learning to read. Some of these clues are: left-to-right directional movement, picture and context clues, configuration, and structural and phonetic analysis of words.

To show children the direction in which words must be read, the

---

[4] Yvonne M. Lofthouse, "Current Experimentation for Future Primary Reading Programs," *Reading in a Changing Society,* International Reading Association Conference Proceedings, Vol. 4 (New York: Scholastic Magazines, 1959), pp. 175–78.

[5] Dorothy M. Dietrich, "Today's Research: Tomorrow's Readers," *Reading in a Changing Society,* International Reading Association Conference Proceedings, Vol. 4 (New York: Scholastic Magazines, 1959), pp. 232–35.

teacher sweeps her hand along the line of writing from left to right. Such directional guidance in reading words, phrases, and sentences establishes a habit of reading that is necessary for comprehension and for the recognition of correct sequence of letters within words. This directional sweep can also show children that reading is done in thought units and help to avoid word-by-word reading. Without teaching in the left-to-right movement a child may look at words and sentences as he would a picture, where he may choose any place as a starting point. He may then acquire such reversal errors as reading *saw* for *was*.

Picture and context clues are other aids to reading. The pictures in school readers furnish valuable hints as to the story. When the teacher and pupils discuss the pictures, anticipation of the content of the reading material may be aroused. Context clues reveal the meaning of a word or group of words from their relationship to the rest of the sentence. In the sentence, "The dog looked at John with two big eyes," the word *eyes* could be inferred from the fact that dogs cannot look with any other part of the body. Context clues not only aid comprehension but are important time-savers as well.

Still another key to unlocking the mysteries of the printed page is *configuration* or the form of words. Configuration is especially helpful in the present method of teaching children to see words as wholes before any attempt is made at analysis of words. Children learn to distinguish likenesses and differences in the forms of words. They may notice the length of words, the width and height of letters, and the placement in the word of letters of varying height or width. Teachers of beginning reading have observed that children may remember a word that is considerably longer than other words they have previously learned. Likewise it is easier to remember words with letters of varying height than such words as *are* and *was*. In later reading, a child may use word-form clues as a step toward structural analysis.

In structural analysis a child learns how words are built. He looks for familiar forms within the word. Some words, called inflected words, can be analyzed by finding the root of the word, its suffix, and its prefix. The root of the word contains the unit meaning. The suffix and prefix modify the root meaning. Although prefixes and suffixes do not always have a uniform connotation, a knowledge of their common meanings is a valuable help in comprehension. Another kind of structural analysis is syllabication. A child learns that a syllable is a letter or group of letters in which we hear one vowel sound. He discovers some of the principles of syllabication that help him to pronounce and comprehend the word.

When children have not been able to decipher a word by context clues, configuration, or structural analysis, then phonetic analysis may help them to read the word. At one period in the history of the teaching of reading, phonetic instruction was the basic method, but now it is only one of many methods. The phonetic approach is delayed until children have a large and meaningful sight vocabulary. Since phonetics is primarily a system of generalizing about the sounds of letters and combinations of letters, the attention is necessarily upon parts rather than wholes, and for this reason too early a concentration upon small elements of a word might delay the speed as well as the comprehension of reading. In order to use phonetic clues, the child must know the sounds of our language and the symbols that represent those sounds. This is no simple matter because one symbol may represent several sounds. The phonetic sounds and the generalizations about them are learned directly from words themselves and are not taught in isolation. Many words in our language cannot be analyzed phonetically. Children vary in the amount of phonetic instruction that they need. Always phonetic analysis, like other clues to unlocking reading, should be regarded not only as a means to word perception but also as a step toward understanding the thoughts and emotional reactions of writers.

Good reading techniques are taught at appropriate times and in an effective sequence. Teaching recognition of words by a look-and-say method precedes teaching of the analysis of words. From the beginning, children should be accustomed to seek meaning in reading. In group reading the teacher reads a word that gives a child difficulty so that the meaning of the selection will not be lost. Inaccuracies and errors should be corrected by individual teaching and not allowed to become habit. The teacher keeps a notebook handy to jot down individual needs so that an immediate or nearly immediate conference can correct wrong habits.

A child needs certainty in each step of learning to read. Memorization should not precede meaning nor should speed be sought too early.

Good expression in reading comes naturally after meaning is understood. Oral reading should be a natural speech with natural phrasing. In the reading of verse, rhythm is respected as well as natural phrasing. Choral verse speaking aids the slow and the shy children in natural speaking.

In adult life silent reading predominates over oral reading. Also, for most persons meaning is more easily attached to silent reading. Therefore, silent reading is stressed in today's schools and in a daily lesson usually precedes oral reading. The first two grades give more time to oral reading than do later grades. In every grade, children read for significant purposes. Pictures are studied to foretell the contents of a page, and discussion anticipates what the page may contain. Children will read silently to find out a significant detail such as what Dad said about Jack's absence from home. Or they will try to find the solution to a problem, to foresee the outcome, or to discover some other relationships within a story.

In identifying new words, children will find the meaning from the context, then will search for major parts, like prefixes, suffixes, and roots of words. Then, if necessary, they will isolate syllables, and if they need further analysis, they will sound out the words. They will also try transferring from one technique to another until they find a word that fits the context.

Certain techniques of learning to read greatly aid the speed. Skimming is one of these techniques. The child learns to run his eye over the page to locate key words, or to find a central idea or an important detail. Skimming is not only a rapid method of reading but a great time-saver because the reader can locate needed information without reading word by word and line by line. There is some evidence that skimming which precedes a more careful reading is an aid to comprehension because the reader gets a picture of the whole before the parts. He feels the impact of mood or build-up of ideas.

Reading for pleasure is provided through free choice of books in the classroom and library. Oral reading of verse and choral speaking add to the joys of reading.

In the intermediate grades children learn to read newspapers and encyclopedias, to enjoy literature, to proofread, to detect propaganda, and to evaluate the content of their reading. In subject-matter areas like social studies, health, and science, reading becomes a tool for learning.

Diagnostic and remedial reading. Seriously retarded readers are often placed in special classes for instruction in remedial reading. These classes are smaller than average classes and more individual attention can be given each child.

The techniques of instruction do not differ greatly from good teaching of reading to normal classes, but remediation is directed at specific deficiencies. More than one method of teaching reading is used. In addition to the usual visual and auditory approaches, the child may use a kinesthetic method, such as tracing in sand. When the failure to learn to read is caused by an emotional block, the principles of mental hygiene are applied.

Literature. In both poetry and prose, communication that is touched with the art of imagination is called literature. Poetry is usually distinguished from prose by a greater degree of imagination as well as a rhythmical form.

In prose, children's literature may be fairy stories, folk tales, fables, adventure stories, animal tales, and realistic stories. Poetry is read orally in order to hear the sound as well as to enjoy the aesthetic meaning of the poetic lines. Both poems that rhyme and those that do not rhyme are read. Included in children's poetry are narrative, lyrical, and humorous verse. Choral verse speaking adds to the enjoyment of certain types of poetry. Children may suggest various methods of choral verse speaking that they find appropriate to the meaning and mood of the verse. Some variations in choral verse reading are unison speaking, two-part tonal arrangements, and a line for each child.

The primary objective of literature is enjoyment and appreciation. Methods of dissection and extreme analysis are avoided. As children mature, they come to understand the qualities that make great literature. In the first grade, the child reacts contentedly to the teacher's remark, "We enjoyed that story, didn't we?" When the child is more mature, he may like to tell why he likes a particular story. Other evidence of growth in perception is the discovery that character determines plot. When children are led to make discoveries for themselves, literature takes on the lively interest of life itself.

Evaluation of reading. Evaluation of reading, as in other skill subjects, is made through observation and testing. Standardized tests measure comprehension, vocabulary, accuracy, and speed. A discussion of reading tests can be found in Buros' *The Fifth Mental Measurements Yearbook*.[6]

Appraisal will be in terms of all the objectives of reading. The teacher will evaluate not only reading skills but also achievements

---

[6] Oscar K. Buros, *The Fifth Mental Measurements Yearbook* (Highland Park, New Jersey: Gryphon Press, 1959).

such as the following: Children read with comprehension. They foresee consequences. They try to find solutions to problems. They have sensitive impressions with regard to human relations. They read for pleasure.

Spelling. One of the arts needed in communication is accurate spelling. Reading and speech can be aids in spelling. Children often learn to spell by seeing the words in their reading. Clear pronunciation and articulation help to improve spelling.

Objectives of the spelling program. The first objective of the spelling program is the learning of accurate spelling for the purpose of clear communication in writing. The second objective is the acquisition of power to build words so that the individual can spell words independently; this aim includes the development of phonetic skills, practice in use of the dictionary, and the desire to spell correctly.

Methods of teaching and learning spelling. When the language arts are taught as communication, spelling becomes part of the writing program. Children learn to spell words as they need them in their own writing. This method of learning spelling has been called the *incidental* approach, but might better be termed the *functional* approach. It is well known that children can write words correctly in dictated lists but fail to write the same words correctly in written work. When children want to spell in order to communicate accurately, they are more likely to improve in spelling than when such motivation is lacking. Spelling, like writing, is related to all the activities of the pupils in school. As children read, they look and listen and acquire new words in their speaking vocabularies. These words are used in turn in their written work. These words have meaning, and children want to learn the correct spelling in order to convey ideas.

In the functional approach many opportunities for writing and spelling are offered in other subject-matter areas, such as taking notes, preparing outlines and reports, making notebooks, sending for information, thanking for courtesies shown on field trips, printing newspapers, and writing stories.

To those who need it, individual instruction in spelling to improve accuracy and to build spelling power will be given. The children's spelling achievement may be checked against lists in state or county syllabi or other graded lists.

In some classrooms, children keep self-made dictionaries, or alphabetical card files of words they want to use in their own writing. Eventually, reference to the file is no longer necessary because accuracy in the use of these words becomes habit.

Several school subjects such as arithmetic, social studies, science, and health have technical vocabularies that children need to use in writing reports. Not all of these words have a permanent use for the child and memorization of their spelling is unnecessary. Spelling charts containing the technical words may be kept in plain view for the duration of a unit so that the words can be readily seen. Children are not tested for the spelling of these words. In an integrated program children do much writing, and their achievements in spelling, when measured by standardized tests, compare favorably with children who use more conventional methods.

When spelling has been taught in isolation, spelling achievement has been low.[7] Spelling, like any other activity, must be related to children's continuing needs in order to stimulate their interest and effort.

Individualized instruction in spelling is used to meet the varying abilities, needs, and interests of children. Direct instruction may make use of words from the child's own writing, or of words compiled from the writings of children in general. The disadvantages of using words from compiled lists is that the child may be learning words for which he has no immediate need in his writing. The needs for particular words will vary from pupil to pupil.

Research has shown that short daily periods of time devoted to spelling yield approximately as good results as longer periods.[8] For review purposes, distributed practice has been found to be the most effective.

Features of good study programs include understanding of meanings, development of vocabulary, a multi-sensory approach, phonetical and structural analysis of words, and review of words at distributed intervals.

Children will discover a few generalizations or rules that will be an aid in spelling. Only rules that apply to many words and have few exceptions should be learned. Dictionary skills should be taught through use of picture dictionaries and later through standard dictionaries.

---

[7] Virgil Herrick and Leland Jacobs, *Children and the Language Arts* (Englewood Cliffs, New Jersey: Prentice-Hall, Inc., 1955), p. 258.

[8] J. M. Rice, "The Futility of the Spelling Grind," *Forum*, No. 23 (1897), pp. 163–72.

Evaluation in spelling. Evaluation of children's spelling should include not only accuracy in spelling but also the child's active desire to spell correctly as evidenced by proofreading or by his use of the dictionary or spelling file.

Keeping spelling graphs or other records of progress may serve as incentives to further progress. Differences between scores in pre-tests of a unit and final tests are another source of encouragement. Spelling tests in achievement-test batteries help children compare their progress with norms in other schools. However, these spelling tests are not always valid measurements of spelling achievement during a specific time because the test list may not contain the words the children have studied during that time. The important outcome of the spelling program is increasingly efficient power in independent spelling.

Practical writing. No language-arts program would be complete without expression in writing. Writing is the communication of experiences to someone who will read. In the classroom the readers will be the child's own peers and the teacher.

Writing may be classified as either practical or creative. Practical writing is done for utilitarian purposes; creative writing, for expression of an individual's experiences. It is largely through practical writing that principles of written composition are taught—sentence structure, paragraphing, punctuation, and good usage. Occasions for practical writing in the classroom are writing to someone who is absent, thanking for favors, issuing invitations, preparing book reviews, making notes, and organizing reports.

Handwriting. Handwriting is an important skill because it conveys the thoughts and feelings of the writer. When the handwriting can be read, communication succeeds; when the handwriting is illegible, communication fails. Legibility is therefore the primary objective of handwriting. Next to legibility, the determinants of quality are letter formation, compactness of spacing, and regularity of slant.

Speed in handwriting may interfere with legibility. For this reason, speed in handwriting is not greatly stressed in the elementary school. In today's schools, individuality (or character) is encouraged instead of rigid standards of perfection.

In beginning handwriting, the child writes simple sentences to convey a message. This gives him a motive for writing. In order to write at an early age, the young child uses a simplified form of writing called *manuscript writing*.

A change to cursive writing is usually made at the end of the second grade or the beginning of the third. The pupil progresses best when he himself has learned to diagnose his handwriting and to seek improvement.

Foreign languages. Foreign language instruction, relatively unknown in our public elementary schools until 1952, spread rapidly between 1953 and 1956. At the end of this three-year period, the enrollment in foreign-language classes had increased 500 per cent. In the fall of 1955, German was taught in 40 communities; French, in 192; Spanish, in 203. Some schools reported the teaching of Italian, Norwegian, Japanese, Modern Greek, and Swedish. Still other school children were receiving foreign language instruction through radio and television programs.[9]

Several factors helped to bring about this rapid introduction of foreign languages into the elementary school. The most immediate factor was a conference on "The Role of Foreign Languages in American Schools" on January 15 and 16, 1953, sponsored jointly by the United States Office of Education, the Modern Language Association, and other organizations.[10]

Up to the date of the conference, instruction in language skills had been offered largely in high schools and universities at an age when a spoken language is learned with relative difficulty. The conference encouraged the teaching of a second language in the elementary school.

The objectives of a foreign-language program are an understanding and appreciation of the culture in which the language is spoken and the speaking, reading, and writing of the language.

Foreign-language instruction is usually introduced in grades three or four, but some schools begin the teaching in grade one. A few schools offer a foreign language as an enrichment program for the gifted only.

Foreign languages, at least in the primary grades, are taught on an audio-oral basis. Children listen, then speak what they have

---

[9] Emma M. Berkmaier, "Modern Languages," *Encyclopedia of Educational Research* (New York: The Macmillan Company, 1960), p. 870. With permission.
[10] Earl James McGrath, "Foreign Language Instruction in American Schools," *The Modern Language Journal*, Vol. 37, No. 3 (March, 1953), pp. 115–19.

heard. Reading and writing of the language is sometimes introduced in the fifth and sixth grades. Sounds and sound combinations not in the learner's native language are taught by use of recordings as well as by the teacher's voice. Through repetition of sentences, children learn word order and acquire a sense of sentence structure.

Teachers' manuals have largely replaced textbooks. Inspiration and guidance for the program are sometimes furnished by educational television and radio on which a language expert speaks the foreign language. Recordings for beginning units in several foreign languages are available. The classroom teacher integrates the learning of the foreign language into other experiences of the school day.

Some teachers introduce several modern languages to children through units of work on foreign lands. Children learn greetings and common sayings such as those a visitor to a foreign country is most likely to use.

There is no learning of vocabulary lists, conjugation of verbs, or declension of nouns. Instead, the children converse, put on plays, count, sing songs, and play games. In the fifth grade, reading and writing the foreign language may be introduced, depending upon the needs of the children. Because of the recent introduction of the foreign-language program into the elementary schools, evaluative instruments for the elementary school are lacking. Evaluation programs are currently in progress at several educational centers.

Social Studies in the Elementary School

The social studies are a broad field in which portions of the social sciences are simplified and rearranged for instructional purposes. The social sciences are the field of scholarly studies that deal with society, usually organized into such areas of learning as geography, science, sociology, philosophy, and anthropology. Social living is a phrase that refers to the practice of democratic living in school and society.

The introduction of social studies as a fused study is a contribution of the twentieth century. Formerly history, geography, and civics were taught as separate subjects. It became necessary to extend children's learning to newer fields of the social sciences. The challenge for the teacher is to provide a balanced selection of those skills, generalizations, and values that will most effectively teach children to become good citizens.

Objectives of the social studies. Rapid transportation and communication have brought people on the other side of the globe into our daily lives. It becomes necessary for our future citizens to possess as much information as possible about other peoples, in order to understand their cultures and ways of behavior. We need to learn to act in a spirit of good-will toward others. Our highest objective is better human relations in the world.

The objective of better human relations involves many related values: the necessity of settling differences among men by discussion rather than by force, an understanding of the basic similarities among all people, a realization of cause and effect in both the history and geography of a nation, and a feeling of the bonds of a common brotherhood among all peoples of the world.

How potent is the school in the teaching of human relations? The school is not the only teacher of social education; so also is the home, church, press, radio, television, movies, and other community agencies. The public school is a special social environment, selected by society for maintaining and bringing to fruition the ideals and values of the community. The school, in a united effort during the child's entire school years, can be exceedingly effective in weeding out those behavior practices which are unworthy and preserving those which are worthy.

Comprehension of significant values of the culture is one step toward better human relations, but comprehension must be accompanied by vital action. Children must not only know how to conduct themselves; they must be given opportunities to practice good behavior.

Scope and sequence. All the experiences of children in learning and practicing good human relations constitute the curriculum of the social studies. More than in any other subject-matter area, teachers themselves have had a hand in defining the scope and sequence of the social studies. At the time of the introduction of social studies as a broad area of study, so little material was available that teachers took up the challenge of making a curriculum for their schools or school systems. This participation in curriculum-making accounts for some of the enthusiasm shown by teachers for the social studies.

The content and organization of the social studies program vary from one school system to another, but several designs have emerged. One design selects *areas of living* for study. A second plan chooses experiences that move from the immediate neighborhood to far-away countries. A third design starts with social-science generalizations. Under a fourth design, important values of the culture form the starting point around which social-studies activities are built.

The persistent problems of living have been used as one design. These so-called *areas of living* are the social functions in which man engages in order to supply some basic need such as food, housing, clothing, transportation, communication, conservation, government, production, consumption, labor, and management. An attempt is made each year to include a unit from each area of living. The advantage of such a design is that school study assumes a reality because of its closeness to an actual life situation. In some units children can enrich their experiences by trips into the community. When direct community participation is impossible, the school experiences are made to resemble a life situation as closely as possible. The activities are readily adjustable to the maturity levels of children. The disadvantage of exclusive use of a curriculum centered upon areas of living lies in the failure to include such important social learnings as relate to minority groups and foreign cultures. Moreover this pattern of experiences may place undue emphasis upon what men do rather than upon the values that underlie various cultures.

An example of the areas-of-living design for the social studies is found in the Maryland state program which focuses on six areas of living: (1) family living, (2) citizenship, (3) production, consumption, conservation, and distribution, (4) communication and transportation, (5) recreation, and (6) moral, spiritual, and aesthetic development and expression.[11] Each grade studies one unit from each of these areas of living.

A second social-studies pattern that has become very popular follows a near-to-the-far organization. This pattern begins with the child's own environment and expands to include other lands and people. Whenever a particular continent is selected for study, the trend is toward a concentrated study of one or two countries of that continent rather than upon all its countries. A present trend is emphasis upon the culture of a people and upon relationships of one country to other countries in the world.

---

[11] The Maryland State Department of Education, *Social Studies* (Baltimore: The Department, 1956), p. 13.

A social-studies program that moves from the near to the far is the one suggested by the South Carolina Department of Education *Guide*. The suggested areas for study are:

> Grade 1: Living Togther in Home and School.
> Grade 2: Living Together in the Neighborhood and Community —Community Helpers.
> Grade 3: Expanding Community Life—Occupations and Community Services.
> Grade 4: Living in Typical Regions of South Carolina as Related to Living in Typical Regions of the World.
> Grade 5: Living in the United States, Present and Past.
> Grade 6: Life in Other Countries of the Americas as Related to Life in the United States.[12]

A third approach to building a social-studies scope and sequence is a compilation of generalizations of the various social sciences that children ought to know. In practice, children are given social experiences so that they themselves can discover these generalizations. Abstractions of this kind require a high order of thinking.

To obtain a framework for the social-studies program, the California State Central Committee asked social scientists of California's colleges and universities for lists of concepts from their disciplines that they considered "essential for competent citizenship in our society." The committee made a final list of 18 concepts that were adjusted to meet the maturity levels of elementary school children.[13] To aid teachers in the analysis of a specific generalization, a series of Doctors' theses from Stanford University, such as the one by Peck on aesthetic needs, should prove helpful.[14]

A fourth plan for curriculum-making in the social studies is to compile the major moral and ethical values that are considered most worthy by our society, and to provide experiences in which these values can be practiced. The advantages of this type of curriculum plan lie in the direct application of values to school experiences and in the repetitive applications in grade after grade.

This plan for curriculum-making in the social studies is illustrated

---

[12] South Carolina State Department of Education, *Guide for Teaching of Social Studies* (Columbia: The Department, 1956).

[13] California State Department of Education, *Building Curriculum in Social Studies for the Public Schools of California* (Sacramento: The Department, 1957), pp. 13–49.

[14] Albert D. Peck, *Social Science Generalizations for Use in the Social Studies Curriculum: Expressing and Satisfying Aesthetic Needs and Impulses* (Doctor's Thesis, Stanford: Stanford University, 1958).

by a chart from the Florida State Department of Education. This chart shows how children's school experiences can grow directly out of moral and ethical values. Florida's social-studies program for elementary school children groups these values as follows: growth in meeting self-needs, growth in adjustment to others, and growth in interests.[15]

Units of work in the social studies. In presenting a social-studies unit to a group of pupils, teachers will proceed in various ways. They will arouse the interests of their pupils and lead them to propose purposes for the study. To illustrate, let us suppose that a particular grade is to study a unit on a government similar to our own. The teacher will not ask, "What country shall we study?" but rather, "We have several choices; we might study England, Ghana, or Sweden. If you have a preference as to one of these countries, what is the reason for your choice?" After a discussion on the merits of each choice, a vote may be taken as to the majority choice.

As a next step, the teacher asks the children what they would like to know about the government of the country. Purposes for the study are written on the chalk board. One group may want to find the answers to the following questions: What made the people of Sweden democratic? Are they more or less democratic than we are? What provisions, if any, have they made for unemployment, old age benefits, health insurance, a shorter work week, vacations for workers? What does the government do about encouragement of authors, musicians, and artists? Do they have a Congress like our own? How are their representatives elected? How does the government encourage farming and reforesting? What kind of education does the government provide? What relationships does Sweden have with us and with the United Nations?

Children now make preparations for organization into committees which will be responsible for the answers to one or more of these problems. Whenever possible a child's own interests will be considered in forming committees. In this way motivation is ready-made. However, other considerations may govern committee assignments, such as placing children in a certain group in order to meet their needs for friendship. Therefore some teachers ask children to indicate first, second, and third committee preferences.

Children must learn techniques of working in groups. Methods

---

[15] Florida State Department of Education, *Outcomes in Social Studies for Elementary Grades* (Tallahassee: The Department, n.d.).

of procedure such as election of a group leader and secretary are discussed. Some of the questions to be decided by groups are: Who is to get the information and where? How shall the committee report be made to the class? Who shall be responsible for the evaluation?

Activities will include both individual and group projects. The personal report may be in the form of a booklet that reports in organized fashion the findings of the child's research as well as any creative activities such as paintings, musical compositions, stories or poems that the unit may inspire. A unit on Japan inspired one group of children to write *hokku* (three-line imaginative poems). A study of India stimulated children to make original designs for a "Tree of Life" on which blossomed flowers of all kinds. Either as individuals or as a group, children may make murals of activities in a foreign land, put on a play that dramatizes some social-studies situations, and engage in handicrafts related to the unit.

In order to understand human relations in the community, children participate in exhibits, fairs, museums, art galleries, historical celebrations, and community activities through field trips. A wide variety of activities show children the many possible sources of information open to the curious seeker. These excursions into the community may help vivify the social studies and improve attitudes.

During the unit, the arts of various countries are introduced because in the arts are to be found the deepest sensitivities and the highest aspirations of the people. When the children are deeply interested in a project, they will want opportunities for creative expression in writing, music, or art.

Evaluation of the social education of children. To tie together the strands of the social-studies unit, the various committees give reports on their findings. Through these reports the entire class shares the knowledge gained by each group. Before the final presentation of the committee report, each group has decided upon the form of presentation and has consulted the teacher on its organization and potential interest for the class audience. Children may like to celebrate the completion of the unit with a program not only for their own class but also for parents or another school group. Such programs may include several of the activities experienced in the progress of the unit—the singing of songs, dramatizations, rhythmic activities, debating, reporting of facts, and a display of personal achievements.

A final evaluation within the class will answer such questions as:

Was the project worthwhile? Did we accomplish our purposes? What new facts did we learn? What new skills were acquired? Did our behavior improve in habits of work, of gaining friends, of getting along well together? What changes in attitudes occurred?

An important feature of evaluation is the forming of generalizations. These generalizations must be based upon the data and a consideration of whether sufficient data has been gathered to justify the conclusions of the group. Through generalizations children come gradually to see the universe not as a rag-bag of isolated happenings but as related experiences in a unified whole; this is the essence of wisdom.

Teacher evaluation may include testing, the keeping of permanent records, reporting to parents, and reporting to children.

Tests in the social studies may be either of the standardized or the teacher-made type. In general, teacher-made tests, if carefully devised, are to be preferred to tests made by persons outside the school, however expert they may be at test-making, for the teacher alone knows what experiences have transpired in the classroom. Her own tests will include the multiple objectives of the unit of work and not facts alone, as so often happens in standardized tests in the social studies. This is not to say that standardized tests should not be given by a school; they have their own uses, especially in determining the over-all picture of the school as a whole, as compared with other schools where the test has been given. But the standardized test should not be used to test children on material they have had no opportunity to learn, nor should it be used to judge a teacher's competency.

A number of schools keep in their permanent files cumulative records of units completed and textbooks read. Progress in behavioral values are also noted. Negative instances of behavior should not be recorded because children usually move on to better ways of acting. Negative instances, which occur in the lives of every individual, should not be allowed to stand against a child's records.

Religious education. In the history of the United States, separation of church and state has become an established tradition in education. In no way does this imply that schools are irreverent. They teach the basic essentials of morality, love, wonder, and reverence. With a heterogeneous population such as exists in the United States, no other policy would be just to all families or individuals.

Some states by legislative enactment decree that the Bible should be read daily; others have an added stipulation—Bible reading without comment; still others forbid the reading of the Bible; in the remaining states no mention is made of Biblical reading.

The emphasis in modern schools upon appreciating the common characteristics of man, upon recognizing virtues of all cultures, and upon respecting the dignity and worth of man is highly spiritual in character.

Science, Health, and Safety in the Elementary School

The rapid advance of science extends into every elementary school. Many of the applications of science affect the average man as much as they do the scientist. The technological laboratory opens right into our homes and communities. Now, national and international issues arising from the progress of science have stirred the public into an awareness of the importance of the study of science.

Objectives of science education. An enthusiasm has arisen for more teaching of science in the public schools. The scope of science education is as broad as the general objectives of elementary education, which include better human relations and civic responsibility.

More specific expectations of science education are: first, knowledge and insight about the physical environment; second, development of a way of thinking and working called the scientific method; and third, the acquisition of attitudes that are associated with scientific thinking and acting.

In order to interpret the universe, children are taught the concepts and principles discovered by science. Wherever possible, they are led to make these discoveries for themselves. Concept formation can be a valuable tool in science learning. Bruner and others state the following advantages for the selection and use of concepts as a basis for science teaching:

> They reduce the complexity of the environment. They reduce the necessity of constant learning. They are the means by which objects of the environment are identified. They provide direction for instrumental activity. They permit ordering and relating classes of events.[16]

---

[16] Jerome S. Bruner, Jacqueline J. Goodnow, and George A. Austen, *A Study of Thinking* (New York: John Wiley & Sons, Inc., 1956), pp. 12–15. Reprinted with permission.

An early research study on suitable principles of science for the elementary school was that of Robertson, who named 113 science principles which were selected by specialists as worthy goals for instruction in the elementary school.[17] Martin worked on the problem of selection of principles of the biological sciences of importance in general education, and his research developed a total number of 94 generalizations.[18] A somewhat similar study by Leonelli was directed toward the selection of principles of the physical sciences and their grade placement in the elementary school. His findings showed good agreement among a jury of experts in the selection of 70 principles, but no great agreement on the grade placement of those objectives.[19]

In addition to learning science principles that will help interpret the environment, science education teaches children the problem-solving habit that is called the *scientific method*. So important has this way of thinking and working become in our democratic society that scientific-mindedness is considered as much a part of a cultured person as is his appreciation of good literature.

Still another objective of science education is concerned with forming attitudes associated with the scientific method. Some of these are the spirit of inquiry, open-mindedness, and objectivity. The spirit of inquiry is found in the questions of young children as to the how's and why's of facts in the environment. The business of the school is to keep alive this spirit of questing and desire for discovery. The scientific method encourages open-mindedness; it teaches children to hold conclusions in abeyance until relevant data has been gathered. It also fosters objectivity; it relies not upon personal feelings or prejudices but upon absolute impartiality in the sifting of facts. Desirable attitudes include developing social responsibility toward scientific discoveries and resources so that science will be used to help rather than harm mankind.

In the nineteenth century, science activities in the elementary school were concerned almost exclusively with nature studies.

---

17 Martin L. Robertson, "The Selection of Principles Suitable as Goals of instruction in the Elementary School," *Science Education*, Vol. 19 (1935), pp. 65–70.

18 W. Edgar Martin, "A Determination of the Principles of the Biological Sciences of Importance for General Education," *Science Education*, 29 (1945), pp. 100–105.

19 Renato Edmund Leonelli, *The Selection and Grade Placement of Physical Science Principles in the Elementary School Curriculum*. (Doctor's Thesis, Boston University, 1953).

General science in the elementary school is distinctly a feature of the twentieth century. Influential in bringing about the change from nature study to general science was the Thirty-First Yearbook of the National Society for the Study of Education.[20]

Scope and sequence of science education. Three types of science programs in the elementary school are the incidental, the use of science objectives as a basis for activities, and integrated units of work.

The incidental approach to the teaching of science relies upon children's immediate interests in the how and why of the environment. This approach makes use of children's own interests as motivation. In Rousseau's *Emile,* where one child with one teacher explored interesting aspects of the environment, an excellent case is made for this type of teaching and learning. A trained teacher will use children's immediate interests as motivation for learning, but will also know that children's interests can be developed. Exclusive use of immediate interests alone would mean a loss of important understandings and future interests.

Many classrooms find a place for science news in the sharing period that introduces each school day. Inventories of prospective national and international science projects can prove a challenge to children's interests. *The UNESCO Chronicle* outlines exciting main trends of inquiry in the field of the natural sciences such as oceanography, meteorology, and research into outer space.[21]

A second method of planning for science programs is the use of science principles as a basis for the science activities. This method represents a present strong trend. Much of the research in the field of elementary science teaching has been in the search for principles of science that are suitable as goals of instruction.

Gerald S. Craig has this to say on the use of principles of science for instructional purposes:

> For years we have recognized the large important principles or conceptions in science have profound influence upon the thinking of people who gain some understanding of them. These principles are so broad and universal that they could be used as large objectives of science instruction. Recently various scientists have utilized the term

---

[20] National Society for the Study of Education, *A Program for Teaching Science,* Thirty-First Yearbook, Part I (Bloomington, Illinois: Public School Publishing Co., 1932).

[21] *UNESCO Chronicle,* Vol. VI, No. 6 (June, 1960), pp. 223–27.

pattern to describe such basic principles as the vastness of space; the age of the earth and the universe; and the universality of change, adaptation, interrelationship, and variation.

Since the best information scientists have at any one time must be revised in keeping with future discoveries, the content of science in the elementary school cannot be considered as set and fixed, even for a few years. Patterns such as those listed above seem to persist as profound descriptive principles from decade to decade in spite of the revisions and modifications that follow new discoveries.[22]

In the third method, science is integrated with other subjects. In these integrated units, children freely explore solutions to a life problem. Material is drawn from all sources of knowledge. Each of the three types of science teaching has its own particular advantages and one type need not be used exclusively.

Methods of teaching and learning science. There is no one best method for a teacher to use in every kind of teaching situation. Teachers of science will do well to incorporate in their teaching some of the procedures of the scientific method. Not all of the formal steps of finding a problem, seeking and sifting data, testing and retesting, and forming generalizations need to be followed in every lesson. The objectivity of science makes its teaching readily adaptable to the use of the scientific method as a way of thinking and working.

The scientific method develops attitudes of wonder, of suspended judgment, of looking at all sides of an issue, of consulting the best authorities, of coming to conclusions based upon the data, and of realizing that conclusions must be tentative in the face of possible future discoveries.

Teachers will offer guidance to pupils in considering what problems are most worthy of study, which authority is better than another, what experiment and retests need to be made, whether to isolate the experimental factor by using a control, when a generalization can be considered a reasonable one, and what applications will serve the general welfare of mankind. Children who are guided in the practice of these attitudes are most likely to form habits of behavior that use these attitudes as part of their daily thinking and ways of behavior.

---

[22] Gerald S. Craig, "What Research Says to the Teacher," *Science in the Elementary Schools,* No. 12 (Washington, D.C.: The National Education Association, 1947), pp. 9–10. Prepared by the American Research Association in cooperation with the Department of Classroom Teachers.

Schools sometimes have their own science laboratories which are available to all classes. Again, some schools have portable science kits that can be brought into the classroom as needed. Wherever possible, experiments are performed by the children. Through performing these experiments themselves, children learn to develop a deftness of hand and a keenness of eye. The classroom has its own museum corner that can be built anew by each group of boys and girls according to their own interests and creative abilities.

Special science classes or clubs are sometimes formed as part of an enrichment program for gifted children. A science project will be pursued more thoroughly by these children than would other children of the same age. Such programs challenge gifted children to work up to their highest potential. These children have much to offer in the way of leadership in the classroom, and for this reason educators believe that the gifted should not be segregated except for relatively brief periods of time.

Science fairs are growing in popularity in many communities. Sometimes exhibits grow out of classroom experiences and again out of individual efforts outside school hours. Some of the most worthwhile exhibits are classroom fairs that are a culmination of the year's work in science. All the children have the fun of participation, and the fair becomes an exciting review of their science learnings.

Evaluation of the science program. Evaluative practices consider the achievement of the primary objectives of the science program: How have children grown in their interpretation of the environment? Do they use their knowledge to control those aspects of the environment over which children of their level of maturity should exercise some degree of control? What kind of attitudes do they exhibit that show growth in objectivity, intellectual honesty, and freedom from superstition?

Children may be tested for certain aspects of the science program, but some of the most important aspects of growth in methods of thinking, in attitudes, and in behavioral changes cannot be measured accurately by pencil-and-paper tests. Teachers observe children's comments that show scientific attitudes such as: "This authority has more recent and more reliable information." "We thought a retest was needed." "We came to some conclusions and checked them by the best authorities we could find." "This conclusion may be an over-generalization." "We think we have omitted an important factor."

The scientifically minded pupil plans ways to discover answers, questions the reliability of data, and evaluates the entire process.

Health and safety. In many schools science and health are taught together. The reason for relating these subjects is that science provides the principles for good health habits. Children develop better health behavior when the underlying reasons for good health behavior are understood. Health education has shifted its emphasis from prescribed, uncritical health rules to scientifically explained reasons for health practices.[23] The rapidly changing discoveries in the area of health make the problem-solving method a better approach than memorization of health facts. It gives practice in making thoughtful choices in regard to health behavior.

The goals of the health program are the child's optimum mental, physical, and emotional health, and better community health. Mental health is fostered by encouraging the child to have confidence in himself. Individual health counseling for continuous growth in healthful living is given by the teacher, the nurse, and the school doctor. This counseling may relate to personal appearance, cleanliness, nutritional needs of the growing child, posture, exercise, and rest. Children help to plan well-balanced meals and to evaluate their own eating habits. Physical education improves motor skills and builds body strengths through participation in rhythm activities, games, and corrective exercises.

Just as health has been integrated with the teaching of science, so also has instruction in safety. Through experiences in problem-solving, children examine the consequences of unsafe and careless action and the reasons for the practice of safety in the home, the school, and the community. They consider safety during fires, storms, and other happenings.

The rapidly moving vehicles of transportation and the frequently congested highways make imperative safety instruction in the crossing of streets, riding in cars and buses, and the use of bicycles. Through sociodrama children enact roles that teach lessons in safety. Vivid instruction is also accomplished through the use of

---

[23] Herbert A. Smith and Kenneth E. Anderson, "Science," *Encyclopedia of Educational Research,* ed. Chester W. Harris (New York: The Macmillan Company, 1960), p. 625. With permission.

films that depict various situations where safe action is needed. The integration of science and safety instruction brings understanding of reasons for carefulness and makes more likely the thoughtful practice of safety.

Arithmetic in the Elementary School

Arithmetic consists of those simple processes and problems of mathematics that are taught at the elementary school level. Arithmetic, like mathematics, is quantitative thinking. Mathematics is to be regarded not as a dead system but as alive and ever growing. Mathematicians believe that future discoveries about number relationships will far surpass those of the past.

Bertrand Russell has defined number as "a bringing together of certain collections, namely, those that have a given number of terms. We can suppose all couples in one bundle, all tens in another, and so on."[24] The modern arithmetic teacher who leads her pupils to see numbers as grouping will recognize the aptness of Russell's definition. This arithmetic grouping is an assemblage of objects or symbols to form a readily perceived arithmetic unit. A well-known example of this type of grouping is the arrangement of spots on dominoes.

Objectives of the arithmetic program. The demands of modern life have exerted a pressure upon the schools for better and more rigorous teaching of arithmetic. The objectives of the arithmetic program are both social and mathematical. We need to teach arithmetic as a reasoning process that has useful applications in daily life as well as in the social and scientific areas of living. The two objectives will not be pursued independently but relatedly. Meaningful conceptions of quantity accompany acquisition of computational skills. Understanding of important mathematical relationships is a necessary prelude to the study of science.

Methods of teaching and learning arithmetic. To meet the objectives of arithmetic instruction in the elementary school, methods of teaching emphasize readiness for learning, meaningful discovery, logical and fused organization, and the social utility of numbers.

The need for a readiness program in arithmetic instruction is ap-

---

24 Bertrand Russell, "Definition of Number," *Introduction to Mathematical Philosophy* (London: George Allen and Unwin Ltd.; New York: The Macmillan Company, 1938), p. 14. With permission.

parent at all levels of the school program. There is no sharp dividing line between children who are ready or those who are not ready. Some are more ready for advanced teaching, others less ready. As compared to other subjects of the school curriculum, arithmetic has a systematic organization which makes it imperative for children to learn some skills before others.

Upon entering school, some children can count to ten; others, to one hundred. Some count by rote without realizing that numbers apply to groups of objects; others count rationally with some understanding of the meaning of numbers as grouping of objects.

In the readiness program the teacher adjusts instruction to meet individual needs. In the primary grades, many experiences with concrete objects are used to show number relationships. The teaching proceeds from the concrete and semi-concrete to the abstract. The readiness program includes experiences in counting, working with manipulative materials in grouping and regrouping, and in reading and writing numbers.

For bright children in all grades, enrichment activities are provided. Some teachers make available to children who wish to use them "enrichment envelopes," each of which contains an arithmetic unit on such subjects as space, money, time, history of numbers, and measurement.

At all levels of arithmetic instruction, children are encouraged to make their own findings about number relationships. Number facts are learned in what is called *block units*. For example, the concept of five is taught by having the child arrange five buttons or five pennies in all the ways that five objects can be grouped. Through their own arrangements of the objects, children learn that 4 and 1; 1 and 4; 3 and 2; 2 and 3; 5 and 0; 0 and 5; 2, 2, and 1—all make 5.

Children move from understanding of numbers through grouping, to knowledge of algorisms. These algorisms are now more than memorized abstractions because they have become meaningful through the children's own discoveries.

Those who have moved gradually from counting, to grouping, to abstract thinking have been found to need less drill than those who do not understand the meaning of the facts they try to memorize. For the best results, practice follows understanding. Then, sufficient repetition is given to assure real mastery in computing accurately and confidently. Children help organize arithmetic facts in a variety of ways and practice the skills at spaced intervals.

Inclusion of arithmetic in units of work is sought to show the daily usefulness of numbers. In these integrated units children also learn to understand the great contributions that mathematics has made to scientific progress, to music, to art, and to economics. From the history of arithmetic, they learn to appreciate the advantages of the Hindu-Arabic number system as compared to some other mathematical system.

The use of mathematics in the child's environment was reported to be one of the major objectives of an action-research project conducted by the New York City Schools. This large-scale project in the development of mathematical understanding is one example of an increasing number of on-the-job research projects in classrooms throughout the nation.

Children may make their own arithmetic kits in which they house materials that will help them discover arithmetic meanings. A cardboard or wooden box will do for the house. The lid of the box may be covered with flannel to serve as a flannel board on which flannel circles can be arranged in various arithmetical designs. The box may contain, as needed, bottle caps, flash cards, colored tooth picks, bundles of sticks (ten to the bundle), clock faces, and fractional parts of circles. Through manipulation of these concrete objects, arithmetic becomes more than an abstract subject.

Other devices for teaching meanings are the abacus, a percentage board, and a hundreds board. Through their own discoveries with concrete objects, children learn the *why* as well as the *how* of numbers. This meaningful learning results in greater retention over a longer period of time and increased ability to solve problems independently.

Graded arithmetic workbooks that contain practice exercises in computational skills and problem-solving are often used in the teaching of arithmetic. The chief advantage in their use is the time saved in providing pupils with carefully graded exercises that need not be copied before solving. A disadvantage of the workbook lies in the fact that the same practice on problems is required by all pupils whether they need the practice or not.

Good workbooks, in addition to other evaluative criteria, will meet children's individual needs for practice. Wise use of these workbooks will include preparatory experiences that stimulate interest and insure meanings before practice is undertaken.

Evaluation of arithmetic. Growth in progress toward arithmetic goals is continuous, and evaluation is a daily necessity. Unless arithmetic errors are corrected, they become habit.

Art and Aesthetics in the Elementary School

It has been often said that all life is art. The wisest philosophers have believed that the whole of life, including mathematics, government, and science, is like music, painting, and the dance. Einstein was once asked a difficult question unrelated to music and replied that he could not give the answer in words but could play it on the violin.

It is impossible to define art with any accuracy but it is essentially man's work. Aesthetics is contemplation of that work. Art is concerned with the creation of beauty, aesthetics with its discovery and appreciation.

No civilization has been considered great unless it has been rich in the creative arts. The arts reflect the culture. In music, painting, and literature are to be found the people's hopes and fears, the yearnings and strivings of the spirit.

All arts, because of the emotional quality inherent in them, have the power of developing not only aesthetic but ethical values as well. Through art, children grow in sensitive feeling and in awareness of beauty around them. They grow too in dreams as their imagination expands.

Our goal in education is not primarily the development of a few great geniuses but rather the encouragement of creativity for the many. Some children will find greater joy and success in one of the creative arts than in another, and therefore the school provides a variety of art experiences.

Creative writing. Creative writing thrives best in a warm atmosphere of acceptance and encouragement. Much freedom is allowed the child in choice of subject and manner of expression. An abundance of facts are needed as the raw material for writing. Children use knowledge of all kinds as a reservoir from which they can draw at will. Children, like great artists, probably attain their best outpourings when the waves of emotion have been stirred. Many teachers use music, art, and literature as a stimulus for creative writing because all of these have the power to release emotion.

At the risk of oversimplification, the process of creativity may be analyzed as impression, assimilation, expression, and aesthetic evaluation.

All the rich experiences of school life may serve as stimuli. Children will be given many experiences in keen perception through the use of sight, hearing, smell, taste, and touch. Children may be inspired to creative expression through reading a book of poetry, listening to great music, or looking at a piece of sculpture. The social studies and science activities may evoke sensitive feelings that seek expression.

The teacher of creative writing is first of all a teacher of inspiration. When children have been stimulated to begin creative writing, the teacher keeps hands off. Each child must now use his own originality. In the process of assimilation, he reconstructs experiences and make new combinations. He groups and regroups, much as in a problem-solving situation. His imagination may come as a flash of sudden insight or as a gradual sensing of relationships. The final product is something that is new for the writer. The distinctive quality of creative work is its uniqueness.

Not all writing is creative. Not all writing brings the joy of true creativity. Some writing is a struggle and an apprenticeship. When the unique expression occurs, the child's face glows with the exaltation which is the touchstone of creativity.

After a child has completed his written expression, his natural expectation is to find an audience for what he has written. Often the young child cannot wait for someone to collect the papers. He eagerly brings the fruit of his achievement to the teacher for appreciation. The teacher warmly accepts every child's work. She finds something to appreciate—some word, some phrase, some bit of colorful perception, or sensitive feeling, or rhythmic form. A child's writing is an expression of his own personality, and rejection of his creative work would be akin to rejection of the self. Children can be trained in good methods of evaluation and be led to discover aesthetic quality in the writing of their peers. With appreciative evaluation by both the child's teacher and his peers, creative writing becomes something the child wants to repeat again and again.

Form and content are inseparable in expression. The teacher does not impose form upon a child's writings because such an imposition limits his freedom of expression. Teachers have observed how an exercise in rhyming may result in stilted and perverted thought.

Many children speak and write in the rhythms of natural conversation. They use a metaphorical language rich in color and feeling. A few illustrations from children's own verse are: "Grass is the whiskers of the earth." "My kitten is striped like a peppermint stick." "The moonlit dogwood made a milkyway in the woods."

Teachers may help children to see metaphorical relationships by such questions as: How did it look to you? How many different ways could we say this? Does this remind you of anything? How is it similar? How is it different?

Creative art. The art program in the elementary school consists of art appreciation and art expression. Children are given experiences in the use of crayons, tempera, water colors, oil paints, clay for modeling, metals, wood, plastics, soap for carving, and textiles. Art activities include making exhibits, dioramas, wall hangings, home-made movies, illustrated book covers, flower arrangements, and attractively arranged bulletin boards.

Creative art, like creative writing, enables the child to grow in self-confidence and power. It provides emotional release in acceptable ways. It spurs the imagination, awakens perception, and enhances the enjoyment of everyday life. The child learns the value of doing something so well that beauty shines in the perfection of the work. He is led by his success to make new discoveries and to go on to new fulfillment. Art helps him achieve stature in his personal development and in his dependability as a citizen who can do his work seriously and well.

Children's art experiences in the elementary school consist of exposure to good art and growth in aesthetic ability. Children's activities may be either individual or group undertakings. Each has its own values. In an individual art experience, the child may express himself freely and uniquely. From this individual activity he feels the growing strength of his own uniqueness. In group work he learns cooperation through adjusting his own ideas to those of others.

Methods of teaching art are classified as the prescriptive method in which children are told what the art activity will be and how it will be done, the creative method in which children are allowed freedom of expression, and the functional procedure in which art and its use are unified. The completely directive method has been largely abandoned in favor of the other two. Almost complete freedom of expression occurs in kindergarten and the first two grades.

Children may need guidance in getting away from stereotyped drawings which they would otherwise continue to make. When a child always draws the same type of house, the teacher, as guide, may say, "You might like to draw your own house or your neighbor's house." Or when the child's figures of human beings always stand stiffly erect, the teacher might ask, "How do children look when they are running?"

Good teaching lies in knowing the developmental steps in art growth and in guidance that does not impose limitations. The developmental stages through which children progress in art are: first, a manipulative stage in which they move a crayon or brush experimentally across a page, sometimes crossing and criss-crossing the lines; second, a seeking of form in which they draw a sky line or a base line on which all objects stand, or in which they show several planes, one above the other; third, a symbolic stage in which a triangle may represent a tree, or a circle may represent a human figure; fourth, an imaginative stage in which the child attempts to tell all he knows, as for example, depicting the inside of a house as well as the outside; fifth, either a realistic or an abstract stage. The realistic artist reproduces objects as they are seen, while the non-realistic artist paints what he feels.

Children's growth will be revealed by the developmental stages of art through which he moves, by his ability to depict meaning through the art product, and by the form in which the child expresses his ideas and feelings. Criteria for form might include the following: Is the child conscious of spacing? Are his figures large or small, according to his purpose? Does he organize and group material? Does he show color balance? Is there dominance of interest? Does he achieve a unity of design? Is he imitative or inventive?

Evaluation considers what is achieved rather than what is not achieved. In evaluating children's art in the classroom, enjoyment of each child's work predominates. The teacher's job is to inspire, to know next steps in growth, and to provide guidance without limiting imagination and originality.

Creative music. Music as an art is very old. Primitive as well as civilized man gave vent to his feelings in song or dance or by use of musical instruments. In today's schools, children engage in numerous musical activities: they sing, dance, play musical instruments, read and use musical notation, and create original music.

The primary objective of music education is enjoyment. Through his own musical performances and creative compositions, the child's spirit is often lifted. Since music comes from many lands, it helps tie knots of friendship with other peoples.

There are many delightful musical activities that can reward the elementary school child. Inasmuch as music must be heard, listening becomes a major technique in learning. Children listen for the sheer pleasure of the rhythms, the melody, the moods, and the appeal to the imagination. Children may listen with planned objectives: to find a repeated melody, to sense the contributions of various musical instruments, or to discern a mood. In group singing, careful listening is needed to unify the singing. The musical rhythm of a dance must be felt before it can be interpreted. Children listen to their own original compositions and learn to value this creativity. Other listening activities include experiences in tempo, dynamics, pitch, and mood. Radio and recordings are used to develop appreciative listening. Listening to music may stimulate the child to some form of creativity in writing, art, or music.

Music may be created by the child in several ways: first, music without words; second, words and music created simultaneously; and third, either music may be fitted to the words or words fitted to the music.

Examples of the first method are spontaneous humming, whistling, or outbursts of song. Again, children discover music on the piano, xylophone, drum, melody flute, bells, water glasses, or autoharps. The notes on some of these musical instruments can be numbered or labelled in musical syllables. Then recording of the notes by the children is simplified.

The second method of composition, that in which thought and form appear simultaneously, may be encouraged by having the children sing musical greetings in the morning or create songs about what they are doing during the day's activities.

In the third method, children may wish to find words for the melodies they have invented. They sing a phrase and suggest the words to fit the music. If they like the combination, they go on to the next phrase.

In the method of setting words to music, children may read a line of verse, then experiment with music that fits the sense of the line and proceed as they find satisfaction with what is already discovered. They write the numbers of the notes above the words in the verse. Next, musical bars are placed before each accented word. Now the notes are transferred to a staff in any key that is comfortable to the children's singing voice.

Learning musical notation through their own need for its use makes the learning more interesting. Children's growth in musical education is developmental. Musical foundations are built step by step.

Appraisal of a child's growth in music includes the extent to which he has developed in appreciation of music, musical composition, musical performance, and musical notation. Evaluation considers the fact that music is not primarily a skill subject. Expectations of musical performance and skill in musical notation are adapted to children's ability to grow. The school does not aim to produce musical geniuses, and too great a stress on skills could dampen appreciation and kill the desire for musical creativity. Musical performance is not chiefly something to measure, but something to enjoy.

CHAPTER IV

Summary

Basic research in sociology, psychology, and philosophy in the late nineteenth and early twentieth centuries combined to revolutionize teaching practices in our elementary schools. Our sociological ideals of the democratic way and the worth of the individual tended to displace authoritarianism. The predominant psychology centered attention upon the wholeness of experience and the field in which learning takes place. From the pragmatic philosophy blossomed a wholesome awareness of the roundedness of experience in which stimulation, assimilation, and expression form a complete whole.

Multiple goals appeared in education along with the recognition that the learning process was a whole in which changes in ethical and moral values, as well as in behavior, occurred along with the acquisition of subject matter. Schools began to teach for improvement in values, behavior, and subject-matter mastery.

Four of the outstanding Europeans who made significant contributions to either the spirit or procedures of American elementary schools were Rousseau, Pestalozzi, Herbart, and Froebel. From Rousseau came a spirit of liberty and a procedure of learning from direct experiences. Pestalozzi gave the schools the object method of instruction, which stressed the use of concrete objects in learning. Procedures inherited from Herbart were similar to the scientific method now being practiced widely in our schools. Froebel's innovation was the kindergarten with its spirit of informality, joy, and socialization that soon spread into the elementary-school classrooms.

The elementary school of today shows these significant trends: meeting the individual differences among children; use of sociometric and projective techniques; attention to the known laws of child growth and development; use of the scientific method of thinking; encouragement of creative teaching; introduction of group processes; self-directive discipline; audio-visual aids and field trips as materials of instruction; measurement and evaluation. To meet children's differences in rates of learning, teachers give separate assignments based upon children's differences in performance. Sociometric techniques reveal friendship patterns, and projective techniques help to solve some of the problems of disturbed children. Through the findings of the child-study movement, teachers understand better the ways in which children grow and develop. The scientific method uses a problem-solving approach to teach children to think and reason. Creative education's great purpose is development of the imagination and the unique qualities that distinguish one personality from another. Children work in large and small groups because of the stimulation that comes from working together and because they learn in group association how to get along together. Discipline has become democratic and increasingly self-directive. Materials of instruction now include audio-visual aids, field trips into the community, and machines for individual teaching. The multiple techniques of evaluation assess the quality of learning as well as its quantitative achievement.

Parents, educators, and others will want to make a thoughtful appraisal of the accomplishments of the graduates of the new schools. Is it possible at the present time to discern a better quality of education than we have yet known? A study would need to be made of these graduates in later life. And indeed, such a study has been conducted. It is called the Eight Year Study, and was conducted by the Progressive Education Association in cooperation with thirty experimental secondary schools and three hundred colleges and universities. College students coming from traditional schools were compared with college students coming from newer-type schools. The conclusions from this lengthy study can be quoted here only in part:

> The students from newer type schools had higher grade averages . . . clear cut superiority in the willingness and ability to think logically and objectively, an active and vital interest in the world about them and [were] more often cooperative, tolerant, and self-directive.[1]

In the relatively short time that our elementary schools have been in existence, the organization of subject matter has taken many

---

[1] Dean Chamberlin, et al., American Education Fellowship, Commission on the Relation of School and College, "Did They Succeed in College?" *Adventure in American Education,* Vol. IV (New York: Harper & Brothers, 1942), pp. 207–208. With permission.

forms: separate subjects taught in isolation from one another, correlation of subjects, integration, the project method, units of work, and broad fields. New purposes have arisen in order to achieve the best possible mental health of children. Do children grow in a healthy sense of their own adequacy? Are they gradually moving in the direction of self-discipline? Is there pupil planning and purposing, shared activities, and evaluation both by the individual and the group? Are pupils learning how to get along well together? Do children feel that they are contributing members of a democratic group? In any type of organization, principles such as these take precedence over form.

Today's teachers, trained in the psychology of child growth, realize that they cannot do the child's thinking for him but must lead him to think for himself. They must guide the child to seek answers for himself. New materials for solving problems must be presented as the child exhausts the possibilities of the old materials.

The 3 R's become not only tools for use in discovering and assimilating the social heritage but are themselves subjects through which children learn significant values.

The language arts are regarded as a social instrument; they are a means of communication between sender and receiver. They involve ideas and the integrity of ideas, feelings and the interpersonal sensitivity of feelings. In such a purposeful language-arts program reading, writing, speaking, and listening become channels for effective communication. Through his achievements, the child acquires a sense of his own worth as well as that of other individuals.

The social studies teach not only skills and knowledge but also attitudes and habits that will make the child a valuable member of society. The child is made an active participant in community relationships so that he may learn the values that lie deep in the culture. Social living in the classroom is practiced all during the school day but receives its own emphasis in the social studies.

The science program helps children to think accurately, to form tentative conclusions, and to find applications of science principles. Children are led to see in their environment forces that can be used for the welfare of man. Science and social thought are interrelated in all good school programs.

Arithmetic emphasizes understanding, reasoning, seeing of relationships, and the social values of numbers. Long regarded as a skill subject, arithmetic now makes a valuable contribution to better living.

The creative arts develop an appreciation of beauty. They provide an acceptable release for the emotions. Through his own creative expression the child grows in powers of the imagination, keener perception of the environment, and an appreciation of children in other lands who, like himself, seek beauty through music, literature, painting, and everyday surroundings. Art, then, joins the other subjects of the elementary school in helping the child toward self-realization and social maturity.

The art of teaching lies in helping the child to aspire, to follow worthy interests, and to appreciate the excellence of workmanship. Under wise guidance, the child grows in independence of thought and action, and he expands in sensitivity of feeling beyond his self-interests to consideration of the welfare of others. The teacher provides an environment where the individual needs of children are met, and every child can grow toward more complete self-realization.

In the light of the rapid changes taking place in our culture, an accurate picture of schools of the future is difficult to glimpse. Some changes, however, are certain to come. Our democratic ideals will force more equal educational opportunities for all children. There will probably be less local control of curriculum and educational policies. Teacher training will extend over a longer period and will include more general education.

Our graded schools will be outdated as ungraded schools take their place. Audio-visual aids will transform teaching of the future. Effective ways will be found to shorten the time between research findings and their application in the classroom. More emphasis will be placed upon the ways that one individual can get along with other individuals. Children will learn not only good attitudes but habits of acting upon them. Freedom will be regarded as a social responsibility as well as the privilege of an individual. Children in the new schools should make citizens with potentialities for greatness of spirit.

All changes in education should work for the good of children and mankind. Reforms of the schools have come and gone, but each has left its mark in progress. Improvement remains. Non-essentials are dropped. As a nation, we are justly proud of our American public schools. Our democracy was predicated upon the ideal of equality for all citizens. Private schools for limited numbers of children were unable to meet the challenge for free equal education for all children. Public schools captured the imagination of our pioneers who foresaw that universal education in public schools was an inevitable necessity in an expanding democracy.

Bibliography

Allport, Gordon W., *Becoming*. New Haven: Yale University Press, 1955.

American Educational Research Association, "The Educational Program, Early and Middle Childhood," *Review of Educational Research*, 29, No. 2 (April, 1953).

Andrews, Gladys, *Creative Rythmic Movement for Children*. Englewood Cliffs, New Jersey: Prentice-Hall, Inc., 1954.

Association for Supervision and Curriculum Development, *Creating a Good Environment for Learning*. 1954 Yearbook, Washington, D.C.: The Association, National Education Association, 1954.

Blough, Glenn O., and Albert J. Huggett, *Elementary School Science and How to Teach It*. New York: Dryden Press, 1951.

Bonner, Hubert, *Group Dynamics*. New York: The Ronald Press Company, 1959.

Burnett, R. Will, *Teaching Science in the Elementary School*. New York: Holt, Rinehart & Winston, Inc., 1954.

Burrows, Alvina Treut, June D. Ferebee, Doris C. Jackson, and Dorothy O. Saunders, *They All Wanted to Write*. Englewood Cliffs, New Jersey: Prentice-Hall, Inc., 1952.

Caswell, Hollis L., and Arthur W. Foshay, *Education in the Elementary School*. 3rd ed., New York: American Book Co., 1957.

Combs, Arthur, and Donald Snygg, *Individual Behavior*, New York: Harper & Brothers, 1959.

Cunningham, Ruth, et al., *Understanding Group Behavior of Boys and Girls*. New York: Teachers College, Columbia University, 1951.

Dewey, John, *Art as Experience*. New York: G. P. Putnam's Sons, 1934.

Dewey, John, *Democracy and Education*. New York: The Macmillan Company, 1938.

Durrell, Donald D., *Improving Reading Instruction*. New York: World Book Company, 1956.

Education Policies Commission, *Moral and Spiritual Values in the Public Schools*. Washington, D.C.: National Education Association, 1951.

Foshay, Arthur W., and Kenneth D. Wann, *Children's Social Values*. New York: Bureau of Publications, Teachers College, Columbia University, 1954.

Glennon, Vincent J., and Clarence W. Hunnicutt, *What Does Research Say About Arithmetic?* Washington, D.C.: Association for Supervision and Curriculum Development, 1958.

Gray, William S., "Teaching of Reading," Encyclopedia of Educational Research. 3rd ed., New York: The Macmillan Company, 1960.

Greene, Harry A., Albert N. Jorgensen, and Raymond J. Gerberich, *Measurement and Evaluation in the Elementary School*. New York: Longmans, Green and Co., Inc., 1953.

Grossnickle, Foster E., and Leo J. Brueckner, *Discovering Meanings in Arithmetic*. New York: Holt, Rinehart & Winston, Inc., 1959.

Hanna, Lavone A., Gladys L. Potter, and Neva Hagaman, *Unit Teaching in the Elementary School*. New York: Holt, Rinehart & Winston, Inc., 1955.

Herrick, Virgil, and Leland Jacobs, *Children and the Language Arts*. Englewood Cliffs, New Jersey: Prentice-Hall, Inc., 1955.

Hill, Wilhelmina, *Social Studies in the Elementary School Program*. Washington, D.C.: U.S. Department of Health, Education, and Welfare, Bulletin No. 5, 1960.

Hilliard, Pauline, *Improving Social Learnings in the Elementary School*. New York: Teachers College, Columbia University, 1954.

Hughes, Marie M., and George I. Sanchez, *Learning a New Language*. Washington, D.C.: Association for Childhood Education International, 1958.

Kearney, Nolan C., "Elementary School Objectives," Report Prepared for the Mid-Century Committee on Outcomes in Elementary Education. New York: Russell Sage Foundation, 1953.

Lee, J. Murray, and Dorris May Lee, *The Child and His Curriculum*. New York: Appleton-Century-Crofts, Inc., 1950.

Lowenfeld, Victor, *Creative and Mental Growth*. New York: The Macmillan Company, 1952.

Macomber, Freeman G., *Principles of Teaching in the Elementary School*. New York: American Book Company, 1954.

McKim, Margaret G., *Guiding Growth in Reading in the Modern Elementary School*. New York: The Macmillan Company, 1955.

Michaelis, John, *Social Studies for Children in a Democracy*. Englewood Cliffs, New Jersey: Prentice-Hall, Inc., 1956.

Miel, Alice, and Peggy Brogan, *More Than Social Studies*. Englewood Cliffs, New Jersey: Prentice-Hall, Inc., 1957.

Mursell, James, "Music Education," *Principles and Programs*. New York: Silver Burdett, 1958.

National Council of Teachers of English, *Language Arts for Today's Children*. New York: Appleton-Century-Crofts, Inc., 1954.

National Society for the Study of Education, *Social Studies in the Elementary School*. 56th Yearbook, Part II, Chicago, Illinois: University of Chicago, 1957.

Ohlsen, Merle M., ed., *Modern Methods in Elementary Education*. New York: Holt, Rinehart & Winston, Inc., 1959.

Otto, Henry J., Hazel Floyd, and Margaret Rouse, *Principles of Elementary Education*. New York: Holt, Rinehart & Winston, Inc., 1955.

Saucier, W. A., *Theory and Practice in the Elementary School*. New York: The Macmillan Company, 1951.

Shane, Harold G., and E. T. McSwain, *Evaluation and the Elementary Curriculum*. New York: Holt, Rinehart & Winston, Inc., 1958.

Spitzer, Herbert F., *Teaching of Arithmetic*. Boston: Houghton Mifflin Company, 1954.

Stendler, Celia B., *Teaching in the Elementary School*. New York: Harcourt, Brace and Company, 1958.

Stratemeyer, Florence B., Margaret G. McKim, and A. Harry Passow, *Developing a Curriculum for Modern Living*. New York: Bureau of Publications, Teachers College, Columbia University, 1957.

Tooze, Ruth and Beatrice Perham Krone, *Literature and Music as Resources for Social Studies*. Englewood Cliffs, New Jersey: Prentice-Hall, Inc., 1955.

Warner, Ruby H., *The Child and His Elementary School World.* Englewood
    Cliffs, New Jersey: Prentice-Hall, Inc., 1958.
Wesley, Edgar Bruce, and Mary A. Adams, *Teaching Social Studies in Ele-
    mentary Schools.* Boston: D. C. Heath and Company, 1952.
Willcockson, Mary, et al., *Social Education of Young Children.* Washington,
    D.C.: National Council for the Social Studies, National Education As-
    sociation, 1956.
Witty, Paul A., "Children, TV and Reading," *Reading Teacher,* II (October,
    1957), 11–16.
Wrightstone, J. Wayne, *Appraisal of Newer Elementary School Practices.*
    New York: Teachers College, Columbia University, 1938.

Index